New Era in the Non-Western World

❧❧❧ NEW ERA IN THE NON-WESTERN WORLD

BY *Vera Micheles Dean, Harry J. Benda, Warren S. Hunsberger, W. Albert Noyes, Jr., Joseph B. Gittler, Cornelis W. de Kiewiet*

Edited by WARREN S. HUNSBERGER

KENNIKAT PRESS
Port Washington, N. Y./London

 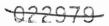

NEW ERA IN THE NON-WESTERN WORLD

Copyright 1957 by Cornell University
Reissued in 1971 by Kennikat Press by arrangement
Library of Congress Catalog Card No: 77-132085
ISBN 0-8046-1413-X

Manufactured by Taylor Publishing Company   Dallas, Texas

ESSAY AND GENERAL LITERATURE INDEX REPRINT SERIES

Preface

MOST of mankind lives and thinks in ways that are unfamiliar to us of the Western world. Until a few years ago, the vast non-Western areas of the earth meant little more to most Americans than faraway places with unpronounceable names. But recent events have forced upon us an awareness of these areas and of the fact that they are important to us. Still, what we know about them is very limited indeed, and our attention is concentrated mostly on matters closer to home. Adequate understanding by Americans of the non-Western world is rarer, more difficult, and more urgent than most of us realize.

The non-West consists of those regions and peoples that are psychologically and culturally, though not always geographically, furthest from North America and Northwest Europe. Airplanes and electronic communications—and now missiles—can reach quickly almost any point on the globe. But the very ease and speed of travel and communication mislead the imagination. We fail to realize how far from us the non-Western peoples are—in the ways they earn a living, in the problems they face day by day, and most of all in their outlook and attitudes.

Our tremendous wealth is one of the principal barriers to our understanding of non-Western peoples. Under the prosperous economic conditions of recent years, the American people have enjoyed a standard of living far above any ever known before in this country or elsewhere. In peace and war alike, the productivity and the incomes of our people have continued to grow rapidly. America's history is one of fabulous success.

Our awareness of this success, our traditional optimism, the comforts we enjoy, and numerous other elements have surrounded us with insulating layers that prevent our seeing or feeling the outer world as it is. This numbing of our senses permits serious misunderstanding even of countries as close to our own as England and France on issues as important as the Suez crisis of 1956. Our ability to understand, or to feel for and with, non-Western peoples is still more limited by the more numerous and greater differences that separate our standard of incomes and comfort, as well as our culture, from theirs.

For persons who have never visited non-Western countries it is very difficult indeed to comprehend the life, the aspirations, and the frustrations of non-Western peoples. What happens in non-Western areas, even though reported accurately by instantaneous means of communication such as the radio and television, does not make the same impression on us as events at home. Just as the earth's atmospheric layers eliminate so much of the physical matter and radiation that bombard the earth from outer space as to leave the human race relatively free of danger from meteors, cosmic rays, or even solar radiation, so also do our cultural protective layers filter information coming from non-Western regions and prevent it from disturbing our complacency.

The American citizen, therefore, needs somehow to penetrate this insulation and to understand things it has prevented from reaching his mind. How can he do so, short of actually living close enough to the peoples and problems concerned to acquire firsthand experience with the realities? This is a challenge to our educational system.

The colleges and universities, which educate our nation's leaders and a growing proportion of our voting public, have the task of equipping their students with receiving apparatus that will enable them to comprehend the forces at work in the non-Western world. Yet today most college graduates lack an adequate awareness of the non-Western world and also the means to appreciate what they hear or read about it.

This need is not filled by the few excellent graduate programs that train a small number of specialists in foreign languages and cultures. Such specialists are necessary, of course, and in fact are far too few for the teaching, research, business, government, and other work that calls for special competence. But specialists do not speak for the electorate and do not control public policy.

Nor do we want national policy on basic issues to be decided solely by technical specialists, no matter how expert they are in their own fields. The people at large must decide these questions if our society is to remain democratic. An important function of specialists is to provide the citizenry with information and interpretation that will enable voters to identify the important issues and to make wise decisions on them.

The University of Rochester has undertaken to deal with this problem through a teaching program aimed principally at the nonspecialist undergraduate. A team of teacher-scholars has been assembled, representing several disciplines and experience in various parts of the non-Western world. The underlying philosophy is that an understanding of the non-West adequate to the needs of the American citizen of today and tomorrow cannot be based on the work of a single discipline such as history, political science, or economics, or on study of a single non-Western area. This philosophy requires a large amount of comparison, of contrast, of synthesis; and group work seems the most effective way to provide these. The Director of this Non-Western Civilizations Program at Rochester is Dr. Vera Micheles Dean, a specialist in the interpretation of international affairs to a wide variety of audiences.

The work of the Rochester group is not confined to undergraduate education. Among its other activities are a special course for high-school teachers and the series of public lectures on which the present volume is based. These lectures, given early in 1957, were addressed to adults but attended by a number of undergraduates and also some high-school students. A second lecture series, on *Continuity and Change in the Non-Western World,* is planned for 1958. Both these series are made possible by grants from the Sidney Hillman Foundation.

Despite the extensive experience of the authors of the papers that follow, many of the ideas here presented are essentially exploratory. The non-Western world requires much fuller Western study. We hope this book will contribute to existing information and interest concerning the non-West, and thus will stimulate study of peoples who, although now close neighbors of ours in certain ways, nevertheless too often remain strangers to us.

Acknowledgment is hereby made for permission to quote from Ernest W. Burgess and Harvey J. Locke's *The Family: From Institution to Companionship,* published by the American Book Company, and from Arthur Waley's *Three Ways of Thought in Ancient China,* published by George Allen and Unwin Ltd.

WARREN S. HUNSBERGER

Rochester, New York
July 1957

Contents

xi

Non-Western Peoples
and the World Community

By VERA MICHELES DEAN

VERA MICHELES DEAN is Director of the Non-Western Civilizations Program and Visiting Professor of Government at the University of Rochester. Born in Russia, she received her A.B. and Ph.D. from Radcliffe, as well as an M.A. from Yale and a number of honorary degrees and awards. A member of the staff of the Foreign Policy Association since 1928, and since 1938 editor of FPA publications, she is a prominent lecturer and writer. Among her books are *The United States and Russia, Europe and the United States, Foreign Policy Without Fear,* and *The Nature of the Non-Western World* (with chapters by Harry J. Benda, Warren S. Hunsberger, and Vernon McKay). During the summer of 1957 she occupied the chair of American History and Institutions at the Graduate School of International Studies, University of New Delhi, teaching "U.S. Foreign Policy in the Twentieth Century."

2

FUTURE historians may decide that one of the most significant developments of the twentieth century was the emergence of the non-Western peoples, comprising two-thirds of the population of the globe, as active participants in the world community. Through this epoch-making change in relations between nations, the twentieth century is witnessing the extension to the world scene of the process of democratization which, in the nineteenth century, took place within national states.

Who are the non-Western peoples? They are the peoples, many of them of ancient lineage and endowed with magnificent civilizations, who have had few, or at most only indirect, contacts with the ideas and forces which shaped what we call Western civilization. Among these ideas and forces are the Greek city-state and the heritage of Greek art and drama; Roman law; the traditions and institutions of Roman Catholic Christianity (as distinguished from Byzantine Christianity, which flourished in Russia and parts of Eastern Europe); the philosophy and the arts of Europe's Middle Ages; the Renaissance and the Reformation; the great political, social, and economic revolutions of England, France, and the United States, which molded Western democracy; and most recently the Industrial Revolution, with all its far-reaching implications for the spiritual and technological conditions of modern society. If we adopt this touchstone, the areas which have developed for the most part outside the orbit of Western civilization include the U.S.S.R., the Middle East, Asia, Africa, and even Latin America, which, although it has been deeply influenced by Catholic Christianity and is geographically part of the Western Hemisphere, nevertheless faces many of the same problems as non-Western nations and has a wide range of common experiences and outlooks.

This does not mean that the non-Western sector of the world is a monolithic block of peoples sharply separated from the Western sector by some kind of curtain. There is as much—and perhaps even more—diversity among non-Western peoples as among the peoples of the West: diversity of religions, of traditions, of political, economic, and social organizations. Nor is the non-West hostile to Western ideas and institutions. Far from it. Over the centuries there has been fruitful cross fertilization between West and non-West—in art and literature, in philosophy and religion, in the skills of administration and of technological know-how. Both sectors have been stimulated and enriched by these exchanges, which modern communications and the growing sense of interdependence have greatly accelerated in the wake of two world wars.

Yet it is important—in fact, in the nuclear age, it is a

life and death matter—for us in the United States to understand the fundamental difference which often creates misunderstandings between West and non-West. This difference is not in the first instance a matter of religion, or ideologies, or race. It is due to the actual, visible difference in the time factor of the development of the Western and non-Western peoples.

By the clock and by the calendar we all seem to be living at approximately the same time in history—in the second half of the twentieth century. Yet in actuality the world lives in many centuries at one and the same moment. As we girdle the globe we can see that while some peoples—the Atlantic community and Australasia—are in the twentieth century, others live all the way from the stone age in Central Africa through the still feudal societies of the Middle East and the medieval villages of Southeast Asia into the modern era of industrialized Japan.

More startling, even within a single nation we find several centuries side by side. To give but one example, Russia's autocratic political system, with Stalin when he was alive as an unchallenged tyrant, reminds one of England and France in the days of Henry VIII and Louis XIV. Its economy, still in the throes of transition from a backward agrarian society to complex modern industry, displays some of the maladjustments of nineteenth-century industrialization in England and the United States. Yet when it comes to scientific knowledge Russia is neck and neck with the most advanced nations of the West in the capacity to use nuclear energy for purposes of war and peace.

When we see the frightening slums of Calcutta, or the shortages of consumer goods in Russia, or the cruelty of the Mau Mau in Kenya and of the World War II Japanese in the Philippines, or the political instability of the Middle East and Latin America, we are apt to think of non-Western peoples as "backward" (an unpleasant phrase connoting mental retardation) or "underdeveloped" (somewhat less invidious, yet suggesting stunted or delayed growth).

If we are to understand the problems of the non-Western peoples, and of our relations with them, we must remember that many of them had flourishing, highly developed civilizations when our ancestors were unknown to history. For a variety of circumstances they passed through periods of eclipse, only to re-emerge with fresh vitality into a world where the West's technological advances confronted them with new challenges. We must resist the temptation to judge non-Western peoples solely by technological standards. Plumbing and electricity, desirable as they may be, are not the only tests of civilization. We must also become aware of the rich contributions the non-Western peoples have made and continue to make to the world's cultural treasure-trove.

As the non-Western peoples, many of whom have achieved freedom from colonial rule only since World War II, belatedly come onto the world stage, they face a fourfold dilemma. Their dilemma is that they (1) seek independence; (2) are aware of and troubled by their continuing dependence; (3) feel the need for interdependence; and (4) are determined to achieve equality in the world community.

Political independence does not in itself lead to or assure economic independence, which in turn, relative as it is for all nations, can be achieved only by a series of political and social changes. These changes can be brought about most effectively through interdependence with the

6

West. Yet a long, and often harsh, experience with Western colonialism, makes the newly liberated non-Western peoples apprehensive about co-operation with the West unless they are certain that the new relationship, in contrast to colonialism, will be that of equals and not of subjects.

First of all, then, the non-Western peoples are determined to achieve political independence from the Western colonial powers. Many of them have reached this goal during the decade since World War II which has seen 570 million of the 700 million ruled by Western nations in 1945 attain independence or self-government. Others became free in 1957—notably Ghana, the first African nation to do so in modern times, and Malaya. Still others look to independence in the foreseeable future, among them Nigeria.

Where independence has come about through more or less voluntary withdrawal by the Western ruler, as in the Philippines, India, Pakistan, Burma, Ceylon, Tunisia, Morocco, and Ghana, relations between the ruler and the ruled have been strengthened by the change in relationship. Where the ruler has resisted the drive for independence, as in Indonesia, Indochina, or Algeria, bitter conflicts, breaking out on occasion into open warfare, have occurred. But even under the best of circumstances the newly liberated non-Western people discovers, the morning after, that political independence does not automatically bring economic improvement or security against outside pressure or attack.

The weakness of the West's policy thus far has been its assumption that the moment the non-Western peoples are freed of colonial rule they will forget their experience

7

with colonialism and unquestioningly accept the Western view of world affairs. It would be wise for Americans to remember that it has taken nearly two centuries for this nation, born out of revolution against British colonial domination, to overcome its opposition to colonialism. If we bear our own experience in mind, not only shall we be more patient with non-Western peoples, we shall consider it a miracle that they have so little ill will toward their recent foreign rulers who had come from the West.

The non-Western nations' fear of a new form of colonialism is reflected in their foreign policies. They are passing through the stage of nationalism which the Western peoples experienced a hundred or more years ago but have by no means yet left behind. What we often call their anti-Westernism is actually antiforeignism—the desire to escape any kind of foreign domination. For the time being it is not directed against Russia, in spite of recent criticism of Russia's ruthless suppression of the Hungarian revolt, for the simple reason that hitherto it has been the Western powers, not Russia, which established colonial empires in Asia, the Middle East, Africa, and Latin America. But antiforeignism can as easily become anti-Russian as anti-Western, if Russia openly attempts to dominate the non-Western nations.

Meanwhile the non-Westerners, for the most part, are reluctant to "choose sides" in the world-wide struggle between the non-Communist coalition led by the United States and the Soviet bloc led by the U.S.S.R. Their policy of "neutralism" has been described by Secretary of State John Foster Dulles as "immoral." Neutralism, however, is not old-fashioned neutrality, that is, abstention from participation in war. Nor does it mean indifference to moral values, or blind acceptance of Communism. In essence, it represents the deep-seated desire of the non-Western peoples, who for one or more centuries have been objects of decisions by Western great powers, to decide their own course in world affairs.

Neutralism is thus a symbol of independence. It also reflects the desire of the non-Western peoples to avoid involvement in war, which, as they see it, would jeopardize their efforts to improve their living standards. To quote Cyrus L. Sulzberger of the *New York Times,* these nations wish "to be neutral and stay alive."

Second, since political independence does not automatically spell economic freedom of action or prosperity, the newly liberated non-Western nations are faced with the necessity of obtaining technical and financial aid from the Western powers whose political rule they have just rejected. Believing, rightly or wrongly, that the colonial rulers had for centuries unfairly exploited their resources for the development of Western economies, they feel justified in asking for Western aid now to carry out what has been well called "the revolution of rising expectations." But still fearful of Western intervention in their economic affairs, they refuse at times to accept aid which is accompanied by political or military conditions—aid "with strings attached." They do not want Russian economic intervention either. But while rejecting Russia's domination, and often opposing native Communists, they are in some cases ready to accept aid from Moscow as well as from the United States and other sources, notably West Germany, which plays an increasingly important part in the development of non-Western areas. From the point of view of the newly liberated peoples, the possibility of obtaining aid from more than one source strengthens their bargaining position with the West. This was illustrated by Egypt's efforts to get arms, and money for the High Aswan Dam, from the West as well as from Russia.

The non-Western peoples, whose political stability and sheer physical survival require at least a modest rise in living standards, are thus torn between the realization that they are still heavily dependent on the West, with its advanced technology and its vast financial resources, and their reluctance, nurtured by long experience of the inequalities of the colonial relationship, to accept the consequences of an economic dependence they find disturbing and irksome. This explains the seemingly ambivalent attitude of many non-Western leaders. On the one hand, they feel that the West has a responsibility for helping them to make the difficult transition from a backward economy to the atomic age as rapidly and painlessly as possible. On the other hand, their national pride makes them sensitive—from the point of view of the Western nations sometimes unduly sensitive—to the slightest hint that Western contributions or investments represent a form of imperialism.

This attitude creates the third aspect of the non-Western dilemma. The newly liberated peoples seek both economic aid and military security through arrangements which transcend relationships with just one or another of the great powers. Fearing to become politically dependent on their former rulers or to be pressured by the U.S.S.R., they tend to rely on the world community as both shield and spear in their relations with the great powers.

Widely diverse as the non-Western peoples are in interests and traditions, they have a common denominator:

that is their fear of political and economic discrimination by the industrially advanced nations. This fear is stronger than their allegiance to regional security blocs such as the Baghdad Pact and the Southeast Asia Treaty Organization (SEATO). This fear holds together the Afro-Asian bloc in the United Nations, which, with 27 votes, now exercises a powerful influence over decisions of the General Assembly on problems regarded as "colonial," and it has forged a link on economic matters between this bloc and the Latin-American countries, hitherto counted on the side of the United States in the United Nations.

The new role of the non-Western peoples in the UN General Assembly, where each member nation, no matter how small or poor, has the same voting strength as the great powers, has alarmed the Western Big Three—the United States, Britain, and France. Western commentators have suggested various ways of reducing the influence of the non-Western group of nations by such methods as "weighted voting" and have complained about the "irresponsibility" of the former colonial peoples. Some have taken the view that the only way of counteracting the non-Western peoples' tendency to oppose the West while adopting a "neutralist" attitude toward Russia and to favor the side of the "colonial" nations is to settle controversial issues, such as the Israeli-Arab conflict, through secret diplomacy outside the United Nations.

But here arises the fourth aspect of the dilemma. It is no longer possible today to exclude the non-Western peoples from full and equal participation in the activities of the world community of which they automatically become a part upon achieving nationhood. Some regional or partial combinations can prove useful to both West or non-West, such as the Commonwealth, or the proposed French Union, or the Eurafrica now being contemplated by France with its fellow members of the European Economic Community, or the Organization of American States, or the Colombo Plan group of nations. But they cannot replace the world-wide agencies of the United Nations and its surrounding cluster of organizations on food, health, and other matters.

Nor do the various suggestions for giving the politically and technologically more advanced nations of the West greater influence in the United Nations through weighted voting offer a prospect of success. It is understandable that the Western powers, which for some five hundred years have dominated the world scene, find it unpleasant and even alarming to have to share their influence with peoples whom, far into the twentieth century, they were accustomed to regard, because of the color of their skin, as subject, and indeed as inferior, peoples, irrespective of their past achievements.

But even if the smaller or weaker nations were willing to accept a method of UN voting based on the concept of "two weights and two measures," which does not seem within the realm of the possible, it is difficult to see what criterion could be found which would favor the West. If votes are to be measured in terms of population, then the U.S.S.R., India, and China would outrank the United States, Britain, and France. If in terms of resources, then the U.S.S.R. and China would share honors with the United States, leaving Britain and France in the cold. If in terms of intangibles such as education, moral values, and so on, then there might ensue a world debate that could exceed in bitterness the ideological conflicts familiar to us today, and this would bode ill for attempts at co-operation between West and non-West.

If what the West objects to is that the non-Western peoples act "irresponsibly" in the United Nations as contrasted with the allegedly "responsible" attitudes of the Western nations (this criticism is usually made when the non-West questions the West's policies in areas still under colonial rule), then the most effective way of helping non-Western peoples to become responsible is to entrust them with responsibilities in the world community. Let us remember that in a democratic nation like ours the rich, the powerful, and the educated do not have more votes than the poor, the weak, and the ill-informed. One of the basic tenets of democracy is the belief that only by participating in public affairs does the citizen learn how to operate a responsible government.

Sooner or later both West and non-West must recognize that all nations, great and small, rich and poor, advanced and still struggling to develop, need integration with the world community as a whole, as represented by the United Nations. It is in this larger community that the process of democratization on the international level will be achieved. The West will have to accept the fact that the majority of the world's population are and will continue to be non-white and have developed outside the traditions of the Western world. The non-Western peoples, for their part, will have to forego their natural resentment of colonialism and accept the responsibilities of co-operation with their former rulers in a world democratic society. Both West and non-West will then discover that the agencies of the United Nations are the most acceptable instruments for assuring collective security and economic aid, which all peoples will need and will have to share as they pass from the stage of nationhood to that of a close-knit world society.

The central issue of our times is no longer whether there is to be a world community—it is now a fact which cannot be negated or destroyed—but whether there can be morality among nations. This issue arises when the world community is shaken by crises and conflicts—such as Suez, the Hungarian revolt, the Kashmir dispute. In this discussion, too, we need the views, not only of the West, but also of the non-Western nations, which rightly or wrongly have believed in the past that the Western powers equated morality with their national interests.

Have the Afro-Asian nations—and particularly a frequent spokesman on their behalf, India's Prime Minister Nehru—the right to assume a "holier-than-thou" attitude about Algeria or Portuguese colonies in Africa, yet be lukewarm in the case of Hungary or resist UN action on Kashmir? Or are the Afro-Asian nations, for their part, right when they ask why the Western powers are deeply distressed over Hungary but remain surprisingly calm about the killing of 18,000 by the French in Algeria in 1956? Is morality, say some of the Afro-Asians, a matter of race and color? Have not the colonial powers in the past enforced a double standard of morality—and don't they do it even now where their writ still runs?

This debate, which cuts across the lines of existing great power blocs, is poignantly reminiscent of the debate that during World War II rent asunder nations, as well as individual consciences, in Nazi-occupied Europe—particularly in France, already divided before Hitler's invasion.

What is morality? Is it merely a matter of decision for

the individual, with such consequences as it may bring for him, or is there a larger, public morality—of the nation, as in wartime France, or, on a still broader plane, of the international community? Must individuals—and nations —be held accountable for their actions, no matter what their motives, and either be punished or exonerated in accordance with an accepted code of conduct?

This is the crux of the problem. Before there can be a judgment to enforce, there must be a consensus as to what is to be judged as right or wrong. There was no such consensus in wartime France. As Albert Camus puts it in his novel *The Fall*, symbolically describing the Zuider Zee, "There's no saying where it begins or ends. So we are steaming along without any landmark; we can't gauge our speed. . . . It's not navigation but dreaming."

Similarly, as yet there is no consensus in the international community. And a consensus will obviously be much more difficult to achieve in a community of more than 2,600,000,000 people varying widely in traditions, religions, economic and social development, and political experience than it was within a homogeneous nation like France. There are but few landmarks in the vast sea the United Nations charts as it navigates—and many hidden shoals. The law of nations, valuable as far as it goes, is still fragmentary. What there is of it is not always observed even by the most law-abiding great powers. How else explain the reluctance of the United States, Britain, and France, before 1956, at a time when the British still controlled the Suez Zone, to challenge effectively Egypt's closure of Suez to Israeli ships or assert the right of "innocent passage" through the Gulf of Aqaba?

Nor can such law as is observed always be enforced, as

it could be in a sovereign nation, since the members of the United Nations are not yet ready to delegate some of their sovereignty to the world organization, and nations, like individuals, are animated by motives which can only infrequently be described as selfless. They feel it is a matter of survival to assert what they regard as their national interests, and they regard their interests as moral, even if the interests similarly defended by other nations, when clashing with their own, are in their view immoral.

Yet slow as the pace of advance may seem to the impatient who would pull down the house because it is not being built fast enough, the nations composing the world community are moving toward a consensus, a majority opinion of mankind, as to what constitutes just or unjust actions in world affairs. Only when the foundations have thus been laid by West and non-West acting together can we hope to see the emergence of morality among nations. And only then will it become evident that national interests, far from being in conflict with or superior to the United Nations, are inextricably a part of the interests of the world community.

Revolution and Nationalism in the Non-Western World

By HARRY J. BENDA

HARRY J. BENDA is Assistant Professor of History and a participant in the Non-Western Civilizations Program at the University of Rochester. A Czechoslovak by birth, he was in business in Indonesia between 1939 and 1946. He subsequently obtained his B.A. and M.A. degrees at the University of New Zealand and his Ph.D. at Cornell University and taught in both universities. He has written widely on Asian affairs and other problems. His book, *The Crescent and the Rising Sun: Indonesian Islam under the Japanese Occupation, 1942–1945*, is scheduled for publication early in 1958. He is also engaged in the writing of a short political history of Indonesian Islam.

THE vast, non-Western majority of mankind—the peoples of Asia, the Middle East, and Africa—for the past hundred years or so have been experiencing the shock of being uprooted from their traditional moorings. These shocks have accompanied liberation, perhaps, yet they have nonetheless been painful, bewildering, and, above all, humiliating shocks. For many decades the tremors of this gradual adjustment of entire continents to the modern world were barely noticed in the West. Fighting our wars or building our peace, we have suffered a fateful Western myopia that permitted us with bland self-assurance to relegate the affairs of the rest of mankind to the periphery of our consciousness. Since the end of the last war, however, these tremors have suddenly and ceaselessly erupted into widespread and violent convulsions which we can no longer ignore. Once of interest to a mere handful of Western scholars, Asia, the Middle East, and Africa have come to vie for headlines with Western affairs, and domestic news even, in our newspapers.

New Era in the Non-Western World

Our unpreparedness for these perturbing events has, I think, been at least partly responsible for our almost frantic search for a scapegoat on whom to pin the responsibility for these discomforting non-Western explosions. We have found Communism a convincing scapegoat. But Communism, in spite of its impressive successes and gruesome excesses, is not the cause of revolution and nationalism in the non-Western world. Communism is itself in part rather the result, and thus often the beneficiary, of those phenomena. Not that the sinister machinations of the Communist rulers are not willfully accelerating or confounding non-Western change; but even had Marx, Engels, Lenin, and Stalin never lived, Asia, the Middle East, Africa, and even Latin America would almost certainly be finding their way into the headlines and the consciousness of the West in this century. Thus if there is need to understand Communism, there is greater need still to understand this new era confronting the non-Western world—and, indeed, ourselves—today. As we come to know Communism, we must necessarily make negative moves of defense. But knowledge of the non-Western world should induce us to make positive efforts toward co-operation and peace.

Yet our understanding of that world is beset by two initial obstacles. In the first place, the limitations of our vocabulary and of our political experience may tend to obscure, rather than to shed light on, what is taking place so many thousands of geographic and historic miles from us. Words like revolution and nationalism may misleadingly suggest familiar landmarks in a non-Western landscape otherwise largely unfamiliar to the Westerner. Indeed, the word revolution itself has carried an ambiguous connotation in Western history in that it has been used to describe, on the one hand, large-scale yet peaceful social changes, such as the Industrial Revolution, and, in contrast, violent, armed upheavals, such as the French Revolution. Both kinds of revolution—the broad current of change as well as the explosive outbursts which punctuate it—are taking place in the non-Western world today. But even though the non-Western revolution in its widest sense partly represents a repercussion of our own commercial, industrial, and technological "revolution," the course of that non-Western revolution is not necessarily following the pattern of our own transformation.

Again, the fact that Americans, Frenchmen, and Britishers have in centuries past had their own revolutions and still cherish their respective nationalisms does not necessarily render our understanding of revolution and nationalism in the non-Western world any easier. Nor, to take another example, does the specifically American experience with the British imperialism of the eighteenth century and the subsequent legacy of American anticolonialism automatically provide us with the proper intellectual or emotional apparatus required for an understanding of the potent anticolonial and anti-imperialist sentiments among many non-Westerners of today.

The second obstacle is closely connected with the first. It lies in our inclination to cling to the familiar, especially if it exhibits a spectacular surface, even though it may hide a complex of unfamiliar causes. Just because non-Western nationalism speaks in symbols familiar to us we are in danger of taking the surface of non-Western nationalism for the sum total of the non-Western revolution. This is actually true not only of Westerners but also of many non-Westerners experiencing in themselves the violent surge of nationalist sentiment. Nationalism is what we may know most of and hear most about whenever non-Westerners speak among themselves and to the outside world. But like the small visible peak of an iceberg, nationalism is only part of the larger non-Western revolution, not the whole revolution itself.

I hope you will not misinterpret these introductory warnings. I am far from suggesting that there is anything necessarily unfathomable, exotic, or oriental—let alone anything inferior—about the non-Western revolution or non-Western nationalism as such. There exist, indeed, many suggestive parallels between them and their Western counterparts. All I am saying is that we cannot understand these non-Western developments automatically and effortlessly, as if they were completely identical with our own experience. It is to the discussion of the similarities and differences between the experience of West and non-West that I shall now address myself.

If some four hundred years ago a Chinese or an Indian, for example, had suddenly found himself transported to medieval Europe, he would have had little difficulty in feeling at home there. He would have found a Europe largely inhabited by peasants, living in age-old, traditional ways in a subsistence economy strikingly similar to his own society. The fact that medieval life centered around the village and the family would have strongly reminded him of his native land. He would have recognized similarities, too, between the governance of medieval Europe and that of his own country: aristocracies, of whatever name, ruled both, to the virtual exclusion of all other classes. What trade in luxuries there existed, in both Europe and

Asia, was incidental rather than central to the livelihood of the population. And, finally, the all-pervasive tie of medieval Christianity to all aspects of life in the Middle Ages, in particular its stress on the virtues of contemplation and sainthood, combined with its disparagement of material pursuits, might have struck a sympathetic chord in a Hindu, Buddhist, or Confucian visitor to the West.

Thus while Western and non-Western civilizations had, for many centuries, remained isolated from each other by and large, they had developed along rather strikingly similar lines, had given rise to basically similar patterns of life and thought, had, in short, for all their cultural, linguistic, and religious differences, been very much "One World." Just as an Indian or Chinese might easily have found his bearings in fifteenth-century France or England, so a fifteenth-century Frenchman or Britisher might have felt fairly at home in the India or China of his times. Significantly enough, this fundamental similarity also brought with it the fact that what little knowledge Europe then had of the outside world had not led to any feeling of cultural and social superiority of West toward non-West. Not only did the West often admire the East, it did so on the whole with very good reason. For there were great non-Western, especially Asian, civilizations whose cultural, political, and even technological achievements Europeans could not but envy and admire.

Then, however, in the short span of four centuries, the West embarked on a whirlwind change. From a static, agrarian society it rushed through a commercial, then an agrarian, and finally a scientific, industrial, and technological revolution. By the nineteenth century these had combined to give to the West an entirely new social and political fabric, an entirely new system of producing and distributing both goods and wealth, and finally an entirely new way of thinking about man, society, and the state, and, indeed, also about God. Western life, which for a thousand years had centered on the land, now found a new habitat in towns and cities throbbing with commerce and trade; and merchants, adventurers, and missionaries expanded the frontiers of the West to non-Western lands. Aristocracies which for centuries had governed Western man gave way to the man of business as the arbiter of society and democratic government. The peasant and serf of feudal Europe now found himself the laborer in mines and factories; where for generations he had been denied the right to have a voice in his own future, he ultimately found himself not only possessed of a vote in government, but also of new rights as a worker.

Last but by no means least, the Christian Church—itself irreparably torn by the storms of the Reformation—no longer commanded the undisputed allegiance of man in the West. The unity of Western Christendom had given way to the emergent national states of Western Europe; and the citizen of the Christian world of the Middle Ages became the citizen of the modern secular state. Nor did he necessarily remain a Christian in the modern world. New modes of thought, inspired by the phenomenal discoveries of science and technology, often seemed at odds with religious beliefs, and many Europeans and Americans abandoned faith in God in the hope of finding salvation in human reason alone. But believers and nonbelievers alike came to embrace a new and dynamic trust in human progress here on earth, a progress which would automatically flow forth from the unfettered energies and the relentless work of modern Western man.

If a time machine could suddenly bring back to life a medieval European and transport him to the contemporary West, he would be a complete stranger, a displaced person in the truest sense of the word, in a world so thoroughly alien to him that he might barely recognize the roots from which it had sprung. He would have no contact with his own posterity; he would, rather, be confronted by a collision with a new, strange, and bewildering world. It is precisely this kind of collision which has taken place between West and non-West during the past hundred years and which has been the prime cause of the non-Western revolution of today. For it was a West utterly transformed as a result of its development since the Middle Ages, a West profoundly different from the rest of the world, that invaded and imposed itself on the non-Western peoples in the nineteenth century.

What rendered this collision particularly poignant and in many ways tragic was the fact that the nineteenth-century West was not merely transformed, but was at the same time thoroughly imbued with the conviction that its own transformation constituted a claim to Western superiority over all those left behind by the wheel of history. The West was convinced that, somehow, providence had singled it out among all others to lead the world to a richer and more prosperous life—a life, be it noted, carved in the image of the West.

Indeed, to our grandfathers it seemed that with the spread of the West's advanced technology and organization to the less fortunate races on earth, the ideal of "One

World" was about to be realized. Many expected that, as Western trade, Western literacy, and Western Christianity would come to be accepted norms of Asians and Africans, happiness and universal brotherhood would ultimately unite mankind. In the meantime, in any case, the West itself profited immensely from the newly found riches and raw materials of the non-Western world, as well as from access to its seemingly inexhaustible markets for Western industrial goods. This accumulation of wealth—part of which, it is true, may have benefited some among the non-Western peoples also—was, in turn, interpreted as proof that the dynamic expansion of the West was blessed either by divine providence or by the march of progress. The White Man's Burden, the West's Civilizing Mission—these were the terms in which our nineteenth-century forefathers combined profits with morality. They expected the gratitude of the "lesser breeds without the law" in return both for the fringe benefits of the present and for the vision of a happier, richer, and united world of the future.

These were not the dreams of our forebears only. Many, if not most, Westerners have similar attitudes today, even though the reality of non-Western change during the past century should have taught us that these dreams were just that—naïve if noble. One of the noblest of them, that of the rapid spread of Christianity, can be cited as a good example. Yet a century of selfless and self-sacrificing missionary work should convince us that in the foreseeable future there is little hope for large-scale conversion to Christianity among non-Westerners, particularly among the adherents of highly developed non-Western religions. On the contrary, it is quite probable that the non-Western revolution has not infrequently derived great impetus from non-Christian—even anti-Christian—faiths, notably Islam, which today is vigorously competing with Christianity for souls in the non-Western world.

There may be several reasons to account for the limited success of Christianity among non-Westerners. For one thing, nineteenth-century Christianity partook of the general mode of Western thought in that it loudly proclaimed its own superiority over, and irreconcilability to, all "heathenish" creeds. But in so doing it became in the eyes of many non-Westerners the white man's religion rather than the harbinger of Christ's message of universal love. This was especially true in the colonies, where the almost unavoidable identification of Christianity with alien overlordship tended to inhibit native acceptance of the faith on its own merits. For another thing, where Christianity did win non-Western—notably Chinese and Japanese—adherents, they were often made to suffer for having embraced a faith whose abhorrence of native beliefs and practices, no less than its insistence on individual salvation, appeared to threaten age-old familial, communal, and even political loyalties. Social ostracism and—in noncolonial areas—governmental proscription thus not infrequently militated against missionary successes.

Quite apart from these considerations, however, it should also be remembered that the precepts of Christianity were only too often violated by the nominal Christians who brought Western goods and ways to the non-West, thus breeding skepticism toward the intruding religion. Finally, since the nineteenth-century West was no longer an exclusively or even predominantly Christian West, Western secular, rationalist, and scientific ideas have militated against the spread of the Christian faith in the non-Western world. This is not to say that non-Westerners, perhaps even millions of them, may not turn to Christ even yet; but the historian's task is to show why the facile optimism in regard to this matter which has for so long prevailed in the West could not but be disappointed. To a large extent, I think, this disappointment was due to ignorance of the non-Western world, as well as to lack of humility.

Nor is this an isolated example of Western unwillingness to view non-Western peoples in terms of their own experiences rather than in those of our wishful thinking. It is almost the rule that, instead of reacting soberly and intelligently to the divergencies which have, with increasing frequency, arisen between Western dreams and non-Western reality, Westerners are all too often prone to shift the responsibility for their disheartening disappointments on others, in recent times primarily on the Communists. The West's hurt feelings at the alleged "loss" of China is a tragic but typical example of this attitude. In thinking about the non-West, many Westerners are, in short, still beset by the nineteenth-century combination of self-adulation, self-righteousness, condescending benevolence, and missionary zeal—whether religious or secular—which not only blinds them to non-Western developments but which also reinforces the wall of misunderstanding between West and non-West. This is unfortunately true of thousands of well-meaning and well-intentioned men and women involved in humanitarian work or aid missions—private as well as governmental—to non-Western nations today.

At the root of these problems lies the failure to understand that the century-old contact between West and non-West has not led—as it could not lead—to the peaceful assimilation of the non-Western world into Western civilization, let alone to love or friendship for the West. Rather, this contact has either set in motion or at least vastly accelerated a profound and complex transformation in the non-Western world. This transformation amounts to nothing less than a revolution in both the long-range and short-range meanings of the term. This non-Western revolution is not only continuing today, it is in fact assuming ever-greater proportions. We should realize that—irrespective of the dangers presented by Communist infiltration and subversion in Asia, Africa, and the Middle East—our continued and increasing involvement in non-Western affairs is bound to add to the revolutionary ferment. Even such benevolent enterprises as large-scale technical and economic aid cannot escape this paradoxical predicament. The new era in the non-Western world is thus likely to witness revolutionary change rather than a millennium of universal peace, prosperity, and harmony. It is not the fact of revolution so much as the course which that revolution will take that we can still hope to influence by our thinking and acting in the decades to come.

To show why we should not rashly attempt to diagnose the non-Western revolution in terms of our own past, I submit five points of outstanding importance to our understanding of non-Western revolution. In the first place, our revolutions are a thing of the past. Whether we realize it or not, we are the beneficiaries of those revolutions whose memory we cherish but whose realities we no longer know. In particular, we are the beneficiaries of the

postrevolutionary *status quo,* both within our own societies and in a world which these Western revolutions
had been instrumental in temporarily placing under our
domination. But the non-Western revolution is a thing of
the present and the immediate future; its aim is at least
in part to destroy the *status quo* from which the West
has for so long derived such immense benefits. It is doubtful whether our heads are more ready to comprehend
than our hearts are willing to accept this hard truth.

Second, and even more important, we must remember
that the enormous changes wrought in the West by evolution and revolution have been of our own making. Until
this century, at any rate, no significant outside force ever
interfered with these developments, and no alien civilization superimposed its values on the West or dictated the
speed of its change. However far-reaching that change
was, Western man in the end could find himself at home
in, and make peace with, his new environment. Not so in
the non-Western world. Instead of generating dynamic
change from within, it has been subjected to change from
without. In particular, instead of giving rise to an industrial revolution of its own, it has found itself drawn into
that of the West. As a result, the clash between old and
new—whether in highly developed civilizations like China
or in the more primitive settings of some African tribes—
has been far more severe and abrupt than in the West.
Nothing can bridge the gap which the alien transformer
has created in most non-Western societies. Many non-
Westerners have thus become, both literally and figura-
tively, displaced persons in their own native lands.

Third, even though from one point of view four centuries are but a drop in the ocean of history, from another

they were a luxury afforded the West for adapting itself to a changing environment with relative leisure. Since the West itself produced its own transformation without ever completely severing the ties with its own past, and since it had the time to do so gradually and without interference, it could, as it were, absorb the shocks which it had itself generated. Even then it is doubtful whether the Western developments of the last half-century have been —or will be—as readily absorbed as those of the past. Two World Wars, the mass brutality of Nazism, fascism, and Communism, and the profound internal crisis gripping such an important country as France in our day may mark the end of the West's resilience to the shocks produced at home and abroad. But for purposes of the present discussion suffice it to say that, for several centuries at least, it was the West's good fortune that the history of the grand transformation could be written in terms of an evolution only occasionally punctuated by the flames of revolution.

Again, there is no parallel development in the greater part of the non-Western world. The intruding West has carried the nineteenth and twentieth centuries to non-Western peoples, the majority of whom still lived in the fifteenth, so to speak, or whose own development had at any rate not paralleled that of the West since the fifteenth century. Furthermore, neither the prodding of a relentless West nor the non-Western reaction—whether positive or negative—has allowed the non-Western world enough time to readjust itself gradually to the all-pervasive transformation which the modern era demanded. Millions of non-Westerners are not at home in the present world. As a result, this transformation is now assuming an explosive, revolutionary character which overshadows and supersedes that gradualism in social growth which for a long span of time was the West's precious prerogative. And the non-Western revolution is taking place at a time when the West is itself unsettled by the struggle against Communism and the dangers of nuclear warfare.

There is, fourth, yet another ominous discrepancy. Not only have the past 400-odd years brought industrialization and an astounding increase in the wealth of Western nations; but also internal developments within most Western nations have led to an ever-increasing and more equitable distribution of the national income—and of political power—among the several layers of their populations. The spectacular rise to power of the French bourgeoisie after the revolution of the late eighteenth century is as good an example of this process as is, say, the post-Jacksonian coming-of-age of the "common man" in this country. The modern welfare state—with its graduated income tax, social security, unemployment benefits, and even socialized medicine—constitutes another, fortunately peaceful, chapter in this long history of Western readjustment. For some decades now we, the West, have actually subsidized the economically weaker, such as industrial workers and farmers, out of the pockets of the economically stronger, even if these subsidies nowadays ironically mean paying the American farmer for not growing what no one will buy at "reasonable" prices. Since workers and farmers have the vote in our democratic societies, and since their welfare cannot be ignored, Western nations have had to pay this heavy price as the premium for social and political peace.

By contrast, the greater part of the non-Western world has experienced neither industrialization and the ensuing increase in national income nor a progressive democratization of economic and political power. And even where wealth and income have increased recently—as is the case in the oil-extracting countries of Latin America or the Middle East—the distribution of income has not paralleled the Western pattern. It is not only true that the non-Western world on the whole has remained poor. It is also true that the agrarian masses in the non-Western world have, by and large, at best remained poor and politically impotent. At the same time the rich in the non-Western world have tended to become economically richer and politically stronger, without as a rule feeling obligated to subsidize the politically powerless majority of the poor. In most non-Western countries, finally, no middle class has yet come into being which, as in the West, could generate, and subsequently benefit from, economic and political change, and which would prove willing to share its wealth with other classes.

In this century the feeling of economic inferiority vis-à-vis the West continues to be one of the most potent grievances of non-Western leaders, who claim that even though direct Western political control—colonialism—may be on the wane, the West in fact still controls the economic destinies of most non-Western countries, which have to depend on the export of a few specialized agricultural or mineral products for their well-being and, indeed, for the realization of their own hopes of industrialization. Many non-Westerners even blame the lack of social growth in their own countries—in particular the absence of native middle classes—on the West's economic supremacy. They argue that Western industrialism, and more particularly the penetration of Western enterprises

into their countries, have inhibited the growth of an indigenous bourgeoisie. Not unexpectedly, some of them
have increasingly raised the demand that the West extend
its subsidies beyond its own national boundaries, that it
now subsidize not only its own "have-nots" but those of
the non-Western world, as the price for social and political peace in the world community. Whether either the
interpretation of the economic relationship between West
and non-West or the proffered solution to this disparity is
correct or not, we must realize that to a large extent the
non-Western revolution is a revolution against poverty
and against economic dependence to which Western revolutions offer few counterparts.

My fifth point is that the non-Western revolution is
characterized by a peculiar phenomenon of its own, that
is, by a more or less violent reaction against the West.
The term anti-Westernism, which we so often quite misleadingly restrict to the context of the Cold War, has, in
fact, a history which antedates the rise of Communism
by several decades. It is the result, not of Marxism or
Stalinism, but of the unequal relationship that has existed
between West and non-West for at least the last century.
To a large extent, it is a violent reaction against what a
prominent Britisher recently so aptly termed Western
superciliousness toward the non-Western peoples, their
civilizations and institutions. In the eyes of non-Westerners, the white man has carried his proverbial burden with
such disdain, he has been so imbued with his own superiority vis-à-vis everything "native" and "heathenish,"
that he could not but hurt those whom he professed to
benefit.

The crucial point is not that Western colonialism and

imperialism were necessarily all bad and all wrong. Here and there, at least, some among the non-Western peoples may have derived benefits—economic, political, and administrative—from their contact with, and even their subjugation to, the West. Economics apart, it could be more convincingly argued that in some areas Western colonialism appears to have rather paradoxically implanted a desire for constitutionalism, social justice, and democracy which are on the whole lacking in noncolonial parts of the non-Western world. The crucial point is that, even if the economic record of West-non-West relations had been more beneficial than it was, or if colonialism had brought with it markedly higher living and welfare standards, such advantages would in the eyes of most non-Westerners have been purchased at an intolerably high price. Like Westerners, non-Westerners do not, cannot, and should never be expected to live by bread (or rice) alone.

Though the non-Western revolution is to a large extent a revolt against poverty, it is perhaps to an even larger extent a revolt, a protest, against inequality and imposed inferiority. It is not poverty alone, then, which breeds unrest in the non-Western world, but far less tangible factors, such as a yearning for equality of status, a feeling of hurt pride and impotent dependence on the West. This is one reason why economic aid alone—even, as a visiting Asian statesman recently said to our Congress, a Niagara of dollars—will neither be able to save the non-Western world from Communism nor to remove the anti-Western aspect from the non-Western revolution.

The factor of wounded racial dignity has by and large been absent from the course of Western development. Even the American Revolution, which we so blandly proffer as proof of our understanding of the present non-Western convulsion, forms in reality no adequate parallel. For one thing, the American Revolution was not a revolution of have-nots, or a revolt sparked by poverty; rather, it was the assertion of independence of prosperous colonists, sparked by the desire to safeguard their prosperity. More important still, though eighteenth-century Americans rebelled against British imperialism, against taxation without representation, in short against their deprivation of the rights of Englishmen, they were, after all, Englishmen, albeit somewhat naughty and rebellious ones. They had not been stamped with the indelible mark of inferiority of race, color, and even religion, which has marked the relation of white man and colored man for so long. Nor may we ignore another perturbing fact: just as until recently we made little or no distinction between black and brown or yellow, holding them all more or less equally inferior, so now non-Westerners frequently fail to make adequate distinctions among whites of different countries, holding them a priori all guilty of an inveterate superiority complex, whether or not they have, in fact, a record of colonial domination.

In the eyes of many non-Westerners, even the best-intentioned Western aid and counsel may therefore appear like a Trojan horse which at any moment may disgorge the familiar and resented Western impatience, arrogance, and "I-know-better-than-you" attitude: as the poet had one of the Trojans exclaim when the horse appeared on the ramparts of his doomed city, "Whatever it is, I fear the Greeks, even though they come bearing gifts." This is, of course, one of the reasons why non-

Westerners are so often wary of our latest claim to superior knowledge—our view of the nature of the Communist threat. They find it difficult to regard as "The Free World" the West they think they have known so well; they find it difficult to believe that the real danger confronting them is Communist subversion rather than Western control. In understanding the non-Western revolution, we must, therefore, recognize that Westerners and non-Westerners alike are still the prisoners of their antecedent history. Unless we succeed in freeing ourselves from its shackles, we shall encounter difficulty in urging them to ignore their past unequal relations with us.

Let me, finally, add some brief comments on yet another aspect of anti-Westernism in the non-Western world. In the political context, there actually exist two kinds of anti-Westernism which I will here call "positive" and "negative" anti-Westernism. Both kinds can be found in most non-Western countries, though to varying degrees and in varying proportions. Negative anti-Westernism is an intrinsically conservative and defensive attitude. Its proponents, who usually belong to the older generation, resolutely turn their backs on the West and all it stands for. They exhort their countrymen to follow their example, to scorn the alleged materialism of the West and to seek refuge in seclusion and a return to indigenous traditions. Positive anti-Westernism, on the other hand, a paradoxical yet understandable reaction to the Western impact mainly to be found among members of the younger generation, asserts that the non-West's only hope of gaining parity with, if not ultimate superiority over, the West lies in a conscious copying and adopting—or at least adapting—of Western science, technology, and economics and, above all, of Western political forms, institutions, and ideologies.

Almost every non-Western country has thus witnessed, or is still witnessing, an internal conflict between positive and negative anti-Westernism. In both China and Japan, for example, negative anti-Westernism held sway during the first half of the nineteenth century. But after Commodore Perry's forced imposition of foreign trade on Japan, the positive anti-Westerners gained control and proceeded to turn their country into the most Western non-Western state in the world. In China, on the other hand, the issue was ultimately decided in favor of undisputed Westernization only with the Communist seizure of power in 1949. In other areas, like Pakistan and the Middle East, the outcome of the conflict between the two anti-Western groups is even today still in the balance, but it is very likely that there, too, the positive anti-Westerners will in the end win out, more or less completely, with or without bloodshed.

Before I turn to my discussion of nationalism in the non-Western world, it may be useful to summarize quite briefly the five points just raised about the nature of the non-Western revolution. First, this revolution is directed against the *status quo* that resulted from some four centuries of Western supremacy, and this hard fact militates against our automatic understanding and appreciation of the non-Western revolution, since we have been the beneficiaries of that *status quo*. Second, the momentum of change, which in the West had largely stemmed from within, has been imposed on the non-Western world from without; whereas Westerners as a rule have been able to feel at home in their slowly changing environment, in the non-West rapid change has led to serious material and psychological displacement.

Third, the time factor is very different in the two revolutions. Where the West has had some four centuries to adjust to the far-reaching transition from an agrarian to an industrial society, the non-Western world has had a bare century in which to absorb an intruding and dynamic civilization. As a result, the non-Western revolution tends to be of an explosive, rather than of an evolutionary, character. The fourth argument concerns the economic and social discrepancies which have arisen between West and non-West over the past century. The increased wealth which the West gained through industrialization and its advances in more equitable income distribution, as well as its progressive democratization of political power stand in marked contrast to the static poverty, growing economic inequality, and at best uneven democratization of the larger part of the non-Western world. And, finally, there is the element of anti-Westernism in the non-Western revolution—both in the "positive" and "negative" meanings of the term—which is, of course, without counterpart in the West, and which yet constitutes one of its most perturbing and vexing aspects.

The fact that most Westerners have for several generations lived in national states may lead us to the mistaken assumption that nationalism and the national state are, as it were, "natural" phenomena, inherent in the very nature of social and political organization. But, while it is true that in the West states and empires had existed in antiquity and the Middle Ages, the ideology of nationalism as well as the reality of the nation-state, with its alert, literate citizenry, bound to it by unflinching bonds of loyalty, are fairly recent phenomena. Non-Western nationalism, though it is not infrequently nourished by deep roots of racial, cultural, and religious identity and by cherished memories of imperial grandeur, is even more a product of the modern era. More than that, it is a product of the contact between West and non-West, perhaps the most important—but by no means the only— ideological manifestation of what a while ago I termed positive anti-Westernism.

Socialism and, as Professor Toynbee has pointed out, particularly Communism are likewise adaptations of Western ideologies rendered the more explosive not only by the inherently anti-Western goals which they are made to serve in many parts of the non-Western world, but also by the fact that in Asia, Africa, and the Middle East these egalitarian notions precede an era of increased wealth, rather than coming in its wake as was almost invariably the case in the West.

As yet, however, it is nationalism that is serving as the principal rallying point of most non-Western leaders. As the Bandung Conference of Asian and African nations in 1955 so vividly demonstrated, nationalism is, indeed, the most powerful unifying link among peoples who profoundly differ among themselves in their cultures, religious views, languages, and untold other respects. This is in itself a noteworthy phenomenon, since the history of nationalism in the West is more a chronicle of mutual discord than of unity. If there is such unity, then it is largely explained by the negative, anti-Western, anti-colonial content of non-Western nationalism. One need not be a prophet of doom to anticipate that this negative unity may in time, and perhaps before long, weaken, and that the newly independent non-Western nation-states may then find themselves confronted by some of the dissensions and antagonisms which nationalist aspirations have so often brought in their wake elsewhere; in some areas, notably on the Indian subcontinent, such tendencies are unfortunately already observable today.

Three other aspects of non-Western nationalism deserve our attention, even though not one of them is a phenomenon strictly limited to non-Western areas. The first is the negative content of much of non-Western nationalism, its "anti"-element, which has led as prominent an Asian nationalist spokesman as Mr. Nehru to refer to nationalism as a disease—a disease which may be diagnosed as the festering psychological wounds inflicted by prolonged foreign domination. It is, I think, easier for, say, Germans, Italians, and peoples of the successor nations to the Hapsburg monarchy to develop imaginative insights for an understanding of this social malady on account of their own painful experiences of disunity and foreign rule, than for Americans and Britishers, who for centuries have been proud and secure inheritors of national unity and strength. But if we remind ourselves that in times of national crises such as wars our own nationalisms tend to degenerate into blind chauvinism, heavily charged with "anti"-elements against anything foreign and alien, then we will have gained an insight into the often strident nature of non-Western nationalism today, which, in its revolutionary setting, approximates to such a large extent a crisis phenomenon.

Second, in spite of the fact that in Western historical experience the rise of nationalism has often coincided with the growth of constitutional government and democracy, this coincidence is neither automatic nor inevitable in either West or non-West. The nondemocratic and aggressive nationalisms of Nazi Germany, fascist Italy, and prewar Japan should thus warn us against lightheartedly equating nationalist aspirations with political maturation everywhere in the non-Western world. Nor, again, does the mere change from traditional—tribal, feudal, or religious—ideologies to that of nationalism necessarily correspond to significant social and political change within a country. If such a change is confined to a small ruling group, then nationalism does not connote a "new deal" for the bulk of the population. Rather, instead of bridging the gulf between ruler and ruled, nationalism under those conditions only too easily degenerates into empty yet explosive sloganeering and manipulation by the privileged few. This was as true of most of the central and eastern European states a generation ago as it is still true of many Asian, African, Middle-Eastern, and also Latin-American countries today.

The third aspect of non-Western nationalism I would call its "chain reaction" effect. Again, we are not here dealing with anything specifically oriental in nature, even though the old-established nation-states of the West have, on the whole, not been vitally affected by it. What is happening in some parts of the non-West has actually had its parallels, for example, in Central Europe in this century. In both areas nationalism becomes an infection radiating from the larger group to ethnic, religious, or racial subgroups, each in turn claiming for itself the prerogatives of national self-determination which the larger entity has achieved. The division of British India along religious lines into the Indian Republic and Pakistan is one such example; and the "chain reaction" of local nationalisms, largely based on linguistic identities, has continued to plague the Indian Republic to a marked degree ever since independence was attained in 1947. Similar developments can be found in other parts of newly independent Asian and African states. But it is still too early to know whether national integration will ultimately prevail over local or racial separatisms—as has been the case in this country, England, and France—or whether large parts of the non-Western world will suffer the fate of internal "Balkanization" in the years to come. Thus nationalism, in parts of the Western and non-Western worlds, is not necessarily a panacea or an unmixed blessing.

Non-Western nationalism, moreover, poses some very serious and vexing problems without adequate parallels in the West. The attainment of nationalism's supreme goal—independent nationhood—may tend to obscure the existence, if not the acerbity, of these problems. The reason for this danger is not that non-Western nationalism as such is a thing *sui generis,* ominous in its origins and somehow more dangerous than its Western progenitor. It is, rather, that nationalism has been indiscriminately superimposed upon non-Western cultures by non-Western "positive anti-Westerners," who saw in the nation-state of nineteenth-century Europe the epitome of political organization and of political strength. They have transplanted this Western model to non-Western areas, most of which have at best only tangentially shared in the economic, social, and political growth of the West, and few of which have attained real nationhood yet.

Thus, whereas in the West nationalism as a rule formed the culmination of long and varied processes of organic social growth and nation building, in the non-West national independence in our century denotes a beginning, rather than an end, of revolutionary change. This is why I said initially that nationalism is only part of the non-Western revolution, not its substance.

What, then, is the relationship between nationalism and revolution in the non-Western world? Briefly, it is the relationship between an urban-centered, Western-influenced, and largely Western-educated group of leaders, on the one hand, and millions of peasants or pastoralists to whom the ways and thoughts of the West are, as yet, remote, on the other. While it is true that social and political change in both West and non-West has as a rule emanated from cities rather than from the countryside, non-Western cities are playing a far more crucial role as agents of change than cities have played in the West. For in the course of the past century, cities and towns in the non-Western world have undergone profound and rapid transformations caused by the physical and spiritual contact with the West. Whether that contact took place through direct political control or through the less direct means of trading and diplomacy, it has, as it were, turned these urban centers into alien islands in native seas. This is not to assert that the Western impact stopped at city boundaries but, rather, that its velocity and extent have markedly differed between town and country, and that as a result the ensuing repercussions and reactions have differed profoundly between the two. Geographic distance, as yet barely bridged by adequate

systems of communication, has thus been compounded by
social and psychological alienation.

In cities, particularly in capital cities and coastal towns,
an entirely new civilization has come into being. Westerners who came to live there, be it as transients only,
brought with them Western ways: not only buildings,
business enterprises, and clubs, but above all their individualism, energy, organizational talents, and the myriad
other things that make up modern Western life. Side by
side with them, we find a new, strongly imitative, native
class of urbanites, which has adopted many of the out-
ward trappings of Western life and—more important still
—many of the occidental ways of thought, though not, as
a rule, Western Christianity. Since the turn of the century,
these urban islands have tended to drift away from their
traditional native moorings, in dress, in occupations, in
political life, and even in speech. Today's non-Western
urban elites are often more fluent in a Western tongue
than in the vernaculars of their own countries, and that is
true not only in terms of linguistics but also in terms of the
thought patterns which the foreign language evokes and
expresses.

Among this strongly imitative, urban group are the
"positive anti-Westerners," the non-Western Westernizers
—the diplomats, the officials, the officers, the businessmen,
the teachers and students, whom Toynbee has so aptly
called the "human transformers"—who have embraced
Western nationalism as their goal and who today either
are, or are expecting to become, the leaders of the emerg-
ing non-Western states. Yet however decisive their internal and international importance is at this juncture,

these present-day non-Western leaders do not necessarily express the culmination of the non-Western revolution as such.

It is true that the non-Western revolution, particularly in former colonial areas, was fought, and is being fought, under the banner of nationalism. But because of this fact, the attainment of national independence became a promise of immediate abundance and plenty—a promise which nationalism triumphant may have difficulties in redeeming or, rather, which can at best only be redeemed to the few at first. It is the urban leadership which, as a rule, tends to be the most immediate beneficiary of nationalism's victory in terms of political power and social prestige, if not also in terms of material betterment. By contrast, no comparable improvements accrue to the vast majority of the population. Thus the victory of nationalism may, quite paradoxically, lead to a dangerous widening of the gap between city and countryside in some parts of the non-Western world. In the absence of firm economic and political underpinning, nationalism in the non-Western world may therefore not, in itself, be able for long to satisfy the pent-up revolutionary expectations of broad sectors of non-Western societies; and the nationalist leaders of today may be doomed, like sorcerers' apprentices, to watch the tides of revolution, which they themselves were instrumental in unleashing, wash over and past them to a new shore. Therefore the fusion of urban, nationalist elites with the mass of rural populations is the most pressing task confronting the non-Western revolution in the immediate future.

To understand the gap between political independence and social growth we must now briefly turn to the changes which the modern era has slowly and subtly wrought in those peasant societies which—with the exception of Japan—still form the bulk of non-Western populations. These changes have only gradually radiated from urban centers, and even today there are, of course, parts of many non-Western countries which have remained largely unaffected by these tides of change. Much of the transformation among non-Western peasants—and, for that matter, among nonsedentary populations, such as Arab bedouins—stems from international trade which has turned many non-Western countries into exporters of agricultural or mineral products. Often Western enterprises have introduced scientific exploitation methods, as for example in oil extraction, large-scale plantations, and mining operations. All these enterprises have created new employment opportunities. In the course of a few decades, hundreds of thousands of non-Western peasants have thus found themselves confronted with new, Western-style modes of earning a living in a money economy. Many more still have, at least partly, entered such an economy as individual producers for the world market, without leaving their ancestral villages. The importation of Western mass-produced consumer goods, such as cheap clothing, further stimulated the acquisitive desire to earn cash wages or incomes. Finally, industrialization, however modest its advances have so far been in the non-Western world, has called into being new urban working classes, whose mode of life stands in stark contrast to their rural backgrounds.

It is doubtful that these changes have, in fact, brought with them significant rises in the standard of living of non-Western peasants and pastoralists. But the opening up of new economic vistas, the introduction of economic individualism and cash economies, was bound to have far-reaching social and psychological, as well as purely economic, consequences for those involved in these changes. Whatever the attractions and rewards of the new ways of life, they have undermined the traditional communal or tribal bonds which had, for all the social conservatism they represented, for centuries made life meaningful to the vast majority of non-Western peoples. Almost every single Western-style intrusion, including Christianity, has tended to accelerate social disintegration. Economic individualism itself affected the concept of inalienable family ownership; imported consumer goods rendered homecrafts obsolete, thus upsetting age-old economic balances in the villages. Again, the introduction of Western hygiene and preventive medicine, coupled with improved internal security, particularly in colonial areas, brought in its wake serious population pressures, especially in parts of Asia. Not only did peasant life thus become unhinged from its moorings, but the level of living was lowered wherever more people began to press on the land.

Nor was this all. Participation in the international market has intimately linked non-Western countries to the world economy, with the result that trade fluctuations are affecting ever larger numbers of their citizens. Economic crises, such as the world depression of the 1930's, tend to leave millions of non-Western cultivators, laborers, and entrepreneurs uncomprehending victims of changes in distant markets. Not only have most non-Western countries, because of their one-sided reliance on the export of a few staple commodities, experienced great difficulties in cushioning the effects of economic adversity, but efforts at mitigating or redressing at least the worst of these effects by political means have in the past almost everywhere lagged far behind those in Western countries. Thus the agonized cries of the powerless majority of the poor have gone largely unheeded in both colonial areas and in non-Western countries governed by—and for—the indigenous minority of the powerful and rich.

The peasantry suffered from these drastic changes the more profoundly because the erosion of the traditional order involved the breaking up of local government, of traditional ethics, and of religious organizations. Yet this breakdown was not accompanied by a new and viable alternative of social reintegration. The crucial difference between town and countryside all over the non-Western world is, indeed, that in the former, "positive anti-Westernism," especially nationalism, has provided for a fairly large number of people a new vista, new programs, and new goals, whereas in the latter, political and economic change has left a vacuum which independent nationhood cannot, of itself, fill. Although traditional loyalties, village communalism, and barter economies have been too profoundly affected to provide a spiritual haven of refuge to millions of non-Western peasants today, it is significant that it is among peasants, rather than among townsmen, that "negative anti-Westernism"—often expressed in the form of rebellious religious orthodoxy—nowadays is challenging the rule of non-Western urban leaders as it has challenged that of Westerners in the past. Even then, however, it may be ill-defined hopes for a better morrow, rather than a blind urge to return to a rapidly vanishing past, which are having an increasing effect on rural populations in Asia, Africa, and the Middle East. These hopes do not necessarily center exclusively around purely economic goals; although no doubt there is growing impatience with continued poverty, there may be a greater yearning still for a new *modus vivendi,* for a new security, a new meaningful life to take the place of the eroded traditional patterns.

It is to these anxieties, longings, and hopes that nationalist leaders must find answers in the near or distant future. Their nationalism, in order to become identified with the revolutionary expectations of millions of non-Westerners, will have to bridge the gap between city and countryside. This, to be sure, is a stupendous task of nation building, which not only involves an improvement in material conditions and living standards—a slow process even under optimal conditions—but, and perhaps more important still, the creation of a new social order which can fill the void created by the disruptive changes of the past century. Unless this task can be accomplished, however, the vast majority of non-Westerners will not feel at home in their new nation-states, and may then continue their impatient search for an alternative.

It is hazardous to predict whether, when, and along what ways this crucially important task will be attempted in different parts of the non-Western world. In Japan, for example, though the identification between city and countryside within the framework of national unity was attained in the latter half of the nineteenth century, this unity took the form of an authoritarian, military, and aggressive state. In China, on the other hand, the protracted efforts at national integration ultimately ended in failure in the 1940's; integration was then successfully but brutally completed by the Communists who—quite apart from their military successes—had become adept at alluringly promising Chinese peasants and workers, as well as some impatient intellectuals, the certitudes of a new order, a new status, and a new lease on life which China had vainly craved for so long.

The danger thus exists that the integration of nationalism and non-Western revolution may take place under the aegis of totalitarianism, at present particularly of Communism. This danger is especially great wherever the task of bridging the gap between rulers and ruled has barely been attempted and where urban leaders stubbornly continue to place their own economic and political self-interest above the material and spiritual needs of their disfranchised fellow citizens. In such countries, even the most militant anti-Communism, backed though it may be by Western support, cannot forever remain a substitute for the long-delayed task of nation building. It is here, in particular, that the Communists' ability to pose as true revolutionaries, able and willing to identify nationalist aspirations with vague longings for change and improvement, creates grave dangers of infiltration and subversion, which are more formidable threats than those presented by overt Communist aggression.

There are, fortunately, other parts of the non-Western world, especially some Asian and African countries freed from Western colonial rule during the last decade, where a hopeful beginning in national integration has been made along peaceful, constitutional, and democratic lines, and where totalitarian ideologies consequently find a less receptive non-Western audience. Indeed, the success of the nationalist leadership in countries like India—which, in the late Mahatma Gandhi, possessed the greatest of all non-Western leaders capable of bridging the gulf between city and peasantry—Burma, and, more recently, Ghana, may in the long run be of decisive importance in reducing the attractions of Communism in large areas of the non-Western world.

Whatever the means by which the identification of nationalism and non-Western revolution will be attained, in the final analysis it must come, and indeed it can only come, from within. Military considerations apart, the direct influence which the West can exert on these internal non-Western developments can no longer be of decisive importance. Even so, however, the West can still play a significant role by aiding wisely, honorably, and generously those who have embarked, or are genuinely striving to embark, on the task of non-Western nation building in the truest sense of the word. Our most important contribution need not necessarily lie in the fields of military or even economic aid so much as in a psychological readjustment to the new, crucial era of transformation confronting non-Western leaders today. If we can convince these leaders of our earnest readiness to sever the ties with the past and to meet them as equals, then there may be hope that their nationalism will gradually come to shed its inhibiting "anti"-elements, above all its anti-Westernism. This liberation from past apprehensions may, in turn, release new springs of energy, courage, and patience, which are needed to give substance to non-Western nationalism and thus make it the true fulfillment of the non-Western revolution.

Rising Expectations
and Economic Realities

By WARREN S. HUNSBERGER

WARREN S. HUNSBERGER is Haloid Professor of International Economics and Co-ordinator of the Non-Western Civilizations Program at the University of Rochester. After receiving his A.B. and Ph.D. at Yale, he taught at Princeton and the University of New Hampshire before entering the United States Government in 1941 as an economist for the Board of Economic Warfare. As a Naval officer during World War II, he did research and military government work relating to Africa and Japan. In the Department of State from 1945 to 1953, he was Chief of the Japan Research Branch and later Chief of the Division of Research for Far East. He was detailed as a student to the National War College and later as economist to the staff of the President's Materials Policy Commission before assignment to Brazil and Mexico as Point Four Program Officer. He is currently engaged in a broad study of Japan's economic relations with the United States.

T HE comforts and glitter of the industrial West have captured the imaginations of non-Western peoples. American Cadillacs, Kodaks, and Coca-Cola have a great attraction to everyone who discovers them. The Cadillacs are a favorite form of conspicuous consumption for the business and political upper crust in most non-Communist countries. These and other American cars are to be found wherever people can get them. The Kodaks have been seen on so many American G.I.'s and tourists as to seem almost an article of clothing. And Coca-Cola is so widely advertised and distributed that this is probably the best-known trade name in the world.

These are but surface manifestations of profound changes that are taking place in the thinking of non-Western peoples about economic development and about the contribution economics can make to satisfying their wants for things, for power to maintain their newly won or hoped-for independence, and for national and racial recognition. This change in thinking has been called a "revolution of rising expectations." It is one of the most fundamental phenomena of our age. The demand for economic improvement takes different forms in different parts of the non-West. Different peoples have been stirred to different degrees. But the force of these aspirations is such that governments throughout the non-Western world are committed to economic change. Leaders feel compelled to promise their people economic improvement and to adopt policies in pursuit of this goal.

It is one of the shortcomings of thinking in the United States and other Western countries that we pay so little serious attention to this revolutionary force. While we are increasingly aware of the underdeveloped countries, we have not yet taken the trouble to inform ourselves adequately about their problems, interests, and attitudes. One result is that we view the underdeveloped countries in our terms rather than theirs. For quite sound strategic reasons we are pouring substantial aid, mostly military, into certain underdeveloped countries. Our primary concern for a decade has been the struggle with Soviet Russia. The recipient countries themselves are clearly subordinate in our thinking, and their sensitive people recognize this fact.

The United States does not have a carefully considered broad economic policy toward underdeveloped areas, most of which are in the non-Western world, nor do we have a general economic policy toward non-Western countries, most of which are underdeveloped. We have made very few concessions in the field of commercial policy to answer the chorus of pleas for fairer and more stable prices for raw materials, let alone to admit manufactured goods produced by low-wage non-Western labor. And even our aid programs are so immature that the American ambassador to one of the underdeveloped countries not long ago let it be known that he considered the Point Four Program a "boondoggle."

This discussion will deal with the problems of economic development from the point of view of the non-West. This is not a discussion of United States policy, though the problems of underdeveloped areas have many urgent implications for United States policy. The purpose is to focus attention on what appear to be the aspects most essential to a proper understanding by non-Westerners and Western observers alike.

The rising expectations of the non-West, first of all, must be understood as they are. This yearning for change on the part of the majority of mankind springs in large part from a deep sense of grievance against the West. Non-Western peoples, whether colonial, noncolonial, or recently colonial, share in large measure the feeling that the West has done them grave injustice and that much of this injustice continues today. The economic element in this grievance relates to their feeling that they are unfairly exploited in their commerce with all Western countries, imperial powers or not.

No longer do non-Western peoples accept as natural or right an economic arrangement which leaves them poor and without much bargaining power, while the industrial West enjoys the rich fruits of its own science and technology combined with raw materials from non-Western sources. In talking with Asians, Africans, and Latin Americans I have repeatedly been struck by the force of this feeling against the West.

New Era in the Non-Western World

In Latin America one frequently encounters a concept of "economic colonialism" that holds that, even after more than a century of political independence, Latin-American countries are still the economic slaves of the United States and other industrial countries. The reasoning is that in selling primary products to industrial countries in exchange for manufactured goods, nonindustrial countries are dealing in markets where the industrial countries hold monopoly power and take all the benefits. Throughout the non-West this attitude is to be found, and the intensity with which it is often held contrasts sharply with our relative indifference to these complaints. Many non-Westerners do not accept our view that markets reflect forces that are for the most part impersonal and that free markets are generally best for everyone. They tend to look at markets as human institutions manipulated by humans, so far by Westerners, with only a minimum of benefit to non-Westerners.

Even so, there are important differences in the degree to which non-Western peoples either resent the West or yearn to acquire Western gadgets. In Thailand I was told it would be possible to draw a line on the map not very far from the capital city of Bangkok. On one side the people know of Western products and are using and demanding them more and more. But outside this "lipstick and permanent wave circle" the great majority of Thais live their traditional village life, reportedly contented and knowing little of the existence of different ways. In Indonesia, on the other hand, we hear of persons for whom freedom from Dutch rule was expected to include freedom from taxes and even from work. Japanese occupation and the struggle against the Dutch left little opportunity for Indonesians to remain outside their national revolution. Similar experiences have affected most of Asia. The Middle East, Africa, and Latin America are all stirring, in different ways and to different degrees from one area to another. But, increasingly, non-Western nations and their leaders fit the reference to Colonel Nasser when he was described as a man in a hurry.

Non-Western yearnings are often not sharply focused, even though feelings may run high. Motives are mixed. Specific economic aspirations, like better roads or increased production of export goods to pay for necessary foreign machinery, or even the construction of factories, are complicated by such other feelings as opposition to Western private enterprise, insistence on expensive welfare provisions for workers, unwillingness to pay the necessary taxes, or inability of the local or national leadership to agree on priorities. And when particular groups in underdeveloped countries have clear objectives, these may differ sharply from the objectives of other influential groups. The peasant and the landlord have conflicting interests. The wealthy class will seldom have much enthusiasm for heavy taxation to pay for development. Military and prestige expenditures have a way of taking effective priority over development expenditures. One result is that Western governments and Western individual advisers are frequently tempted to throw up their hands in disgust.

Today's economic reality in non-Western areas contrasts sharply with these new aspirations. Age-old poverty, disease, and distress bear down with appalling harshness. Non-Western peoples are mostly peasant farmers. When two sons survive their father, the farm must support two families instead of one, perhaps by being divided, or else one son must seek his fortune elsewhere. In overpopulated countries such subdivision of farms has often gone far beyond the limits of efficiency, but there still remain hordes of unemployed or underemployed. Hundreds of millions of human beings are today suffering even greater distress than has been traditional in their preindustrial societies. Food production in Asia has been growing less rapidly than population, with the result that food supply per person in large areas is now below the prewar level.[1] Considering the low food consumption before World War II, this decline means that hunger is very widespread indeed. Even in Latin America, where total food consumption has increased along with general economic growth, there are patches of serious overpopulation, and some Latin Americans are literally starving.

Health is poor in most non-Western countries. One American who worked on health problems in China shortly after World War II estimates that Chinese outside the cities had an average of twenty intestinal worms each, while the more fortunate city dwellers had an average of six worms each.[2] Poor diet and poor health contribute to short life. Life expectancy at birth in many non-Western areas appears to be less than fifty years, in India less than thirty-five years, as compared with nearly seventy years in most advanced Western countries.[3]

The clearest general economic indicator of all, if reliable figures were available, would be total income per person. Some rough statistics have been published, but before presenting them I must point out that they apply mainly to monetary transactions and tend to understate incomes in the economies and sectors that are less monetized. Further unreality is introduced when income figures are converted into dollars. As a result, existing income figures are no more than very rough approximations. They show for recent years annual production of $50 to $60 a person in Afghanistan, Burma, Pakistan, India, and Indonesia. In the category between $100 and $300 are Ceylon, the Philippines, Japan, Malaya, Brazil, and Colombia. A few countries, including Argentina, Venezuela, and the U.S.S.R., have reached $500 or more, while the United Kingdom has $1,002 and the United States $2,286.[4] Even allowing for wide margins of error, these figures indicate that extreme differences exist between non-Western income levels and ours. These differences constitute an almost insurmountable barrier to mutual understanding.

Starting from such very low present levels, the poorer non-Western countries face tremendous difficulties in their efforts to industrialize. The countries with higher production per person have in most cases taken the difficult initial steps and have already surmounted some of the barriers to continued growth.

What are the requirements for economic growth in these areas? The factors involved may be grouped as natural resources, human resources, and capital. Students of American history find that our country is endowed with extraordinarily, even uniquely, rich resources in all three groups. The non-Western parts of the world, on the other hand, prove on examination to have remarkably poor endowments in many cases.

Natural resources in non-Western countries vary greatly. Most countries have significant quantities of some important resources, and increasingly the industrial West is importing from non-Western areas essential mineral and agricultural products, such as petroleum, rubber, tin, iron ore, copper, manganese, uranium, and thorium. But even the best-endowed non-Western areas lack something, in most cases some of the resources most essential in modern industry. By contrast with the extraordinary quantity, quality, and variety of natural resources found in the United States, most non-Western nations are resource poor. For example, in looking for resource complexes comparable to that of the Pittsburgh area, one finds some zones in Russia and possibly three other regions in the whole of the non-Western world where presently known resources are rich and varied enough to merit this comparison. Elsewhere there are important lacks, such as coal, which is missing from most of Latin America, Southeast Asia, and the Middle East. Or the resources are not accessible to each other or to easy transportation, as in much of Latin America. Or rainfall is inadequate, the terrain forbidding, or the climatic conditions extreme. Industry in non-Western countries must be built on a resource base that is relatively poor in most cases, especially in the most densely populated areas. Development is not made impossible as a consequence, but specialization and foreign trade are made far more necessary by the resultant inability to develop self-sufficiency.

Human resources are even more important than natural resources. In fact, human substance is recognized as the most important factor in the production and development equation. It seems improbable that any country with inadequate human resources can develop very far unless human lacks are somehow made good; but natural resource shortages can be counteracted by foreign trade, as Japan's record clearly shows. In addition to adequate numbers of workers and a wide range of skills, there is urgent need also for managerial talent, technology, and leadership of all kinds. Non-Western countries have important deficiencies here. Unskilled labor is generally available, in most countries usually in great surplus, though the health and social customs of the groups concerned affect importantly their productive capacity. Here in the United States students in elementary economics courses used to be amused at the "backward-sloping labor supply curve" drawn to illustrate the phenomenon of Asian, African, and Latin-American workers who react to a wage increase by working less. But this situation looks less remarkable now, when we Americans, too, are taking some of our increased productivity in the form of a shorter work week and paid vacations. Skilled labor exists in underdeveloped economies, though existing skills apply mostly to handicrafts, and works of impressive beauty may be common; but mechanical and industrial skills tend to be extremely scarce. Scarcest of all are the engineers, higher technicians, inventors, and people to tackle new jobs and make innovations.

These human shortages are partly the result of specific lacks in the recent past, as, for example, the lack of schools and laboratories for training engineers. But far more significant is the social milieu and its tendency to foster—or, in non-Western countries, mostly not to foster —the education and employment of talented people for technology, invention, or business management. Business managers are scarce because in many countries business is looked down upon as less honorable than law, politics, military life, or the priesthood. Engineers and higher technicians are scarce both for this reason and because persons with as much education as engineering requires are loathe to soil their hands in practical application of principles learned. Inventors are scarce for reasons that are more difficult to define precisely but perhaps essentially because most non-Western cultures have not been mechanically oriented and look upon innovation of any kind as undesirable, even if not positively evil.

Leadership is a human resource that is particularly scarce, whether for government, for new enterprises public or private, or for the many other activities that an industrializing society must undertake. The way society tackles a problem varies tremendously from one country to another. Many non-Western cultures have tended to be guided by tradition, as in China, looking to the past for solutions to present problems. Somehow in nineteenth-century Japan there emerged after the opening of trade a new group who displaced the existing leadership and proceeded to industrialize the country by extremely vigorous initiative from the top. New problems were tackled with technical help from Western specialists, by study of Western solutions, and by pragmatic experimentation. This leadership at the top was followed with remarkable success at all lower levels. Nineteenth-century China did not succeed in abandoning tradition sufficiently to devote much attention and talent to the new problems. Only now, under Communist leadership, is China vigorously tackling the problem of industrialization. Other non-Western countries are now approaching the problems of modernization with varying degrees of vigor and success.

The third basic factor in an economy is capital—tools, machinery, and facilities to supplement or displace human muscle and skill. Every economy has some productive capital, but there are very sharp differences between developed and underdeveloped economies with regard to both types and quantities of capital. These differences are related to a country's stage of economic development. An underdeveloped country tends to save very little, generally not more than 5 per cent of total production, and these savings tend to be used inefficiently. (Here capital is defined as past production devoted not to consumption but to present and future production. Saving is the process of diverting from consumption things that are produced, usually in the process changing the character of some of the things produced. Investment is the process of putting to productive uses the things saved.) Developed countries tend to save at least 10 per cent of gross production and often very much more, which they use to replace obsolete and worn tools and the like and to expand the supply of productive facilities. During development, therefore, a major change takes place in habits of saving and investment, and thereafter the higher level of saving tends to continue more or less by momentum. Thus growth becomes self-sustaining, and the attainment of this stage marks an economy's escape from the underdeveloped category.[5]

How then can a poor, underdeveloped country start this process of accumulating the capital necessary for development? For example, what are the sources of savings in India? The 83 per cent of the population that are peasants can save very little, mainly because of their extremely low income, but also because of traditions that lead peasants to spend as much as possible on weddings, funerals, and other festivals. Until these ways change and the Indian peasant is strongly motivated to hold back something for deposit, for improving his farm or village, or for educating his children, it is hard to foresee his making the very severe sacrifices involved. The rich, on the other hand, are very few, and their tradition has been to use their riches in lavish living, with occasional token donations to the poor. No modern industries are created by such activities. But a change is taking place. Luxuries are giving way somewhat to modest living, while some of the income of the wealthy is being invested. The middle class of merchants and others between the very poor and the very rich might be expected to have both the necessary attitudes and enough income to put something aside for productive investment. This process is already taking place, but the pace is very slow because India's middle class is still extremely small.

Voluntary saving, unfortunately, cannot possibly provide all the capital necessary to start the process of development in India or elsewhere, according to the present outlook. Forced saving through taxation or inflationary currency issue is another part of the Indian plan and of the facts of contemporary life elsewhere. But these two sources of capital, attractive as they are to the governments of underdeveloped countries, raise serious problems. The people who are too poor to save voluntarily are also too poor to pay much in taxes unless the government concerned is prepared to be brutal in taking away a large part of the peasant's crops. The Communist regime in China is using such forcible methods. The democratic regime in India has adopted a policy of avoiding crude and brutal force, and Indian taxation and capital accumulation appear to be substantially below Chinese levels. The rich and the middle class are also possible tax sources, and they are being tapped in varying degrees in different underdeveloped countries. India is working relatively efficiently within its framework of consent, but tax income meets only part of total needs. Communist China, like Soviet Russia earlier, has resorted to large-scale expropriation of private wealth, and even liquidation of landowners and other relatively wealthy people. In the Philippines, Indonesia, Latin America, and many other areas, on the other hand, the wealthy few resist taxation very effectively. In any underdeveloped country the creation of an honest, effective, and efficient tax system and administration is a major task, and a very difficult one.

Inflation results by conscious decision or by default in virtually every country attempting rapid development. Nineteenth-century Japan managed to keep inflation from getting out of hand. India since 1947 seems to have kept inflationary forces in check rather successfully, though grave difficulties remain to be solved in financing the Second Five Year Plan (1956-1961). In war-torn Korea inflation has gone very far. In much of Latin America, despite rapid growth in production, inflation is a very serious disrupting factor. The temptation is at times irresistible for weak governments to pay bills simply by printing money. The inflation problem tends to be much more difficult in underdeveloped than in developed countries, and no observer of economic trends in Europe and the United States since World War II can fail to be impressed by the great pressure here.

Capital accumulation by either voluntary or forced saving during the early part of the development process is thus very difficult indeed. But if these efforts result in increasing total production, especially if new enterprises are profitable, then further capital accumulation tends to become progressively easier. A substantial portion of the increased production may be diverted to further increases in productive capacity, by either voluntary or forced saving. And profits can be reinvested, whether earned by private businessmen or by government enterprises. When this reinvestment flow is large, productive capacity can expand rapidly. And as development proceeds, more and more new forms of saving, particularly formalized arrangements involving financial institutions, tend to swell the flow. Insurance, pension plans, endowments, trust funds, and various forms of banking and credit operations, even certain installment buying, all serve to gather funds and channel them into the creation of additional productive facilities. It is when profit reinvestment and these institutional forms of saving become widespread that an economy's growth can become self-sustaining, since the flow of funds for investment then becomes more or less automatic at levels that are very high relative to those of stagnant underdeveloped economies.

This is only a summary sketch of the process of economic development. The difficulties are so many and so great that only a few societies in all human history have reached the stage of self-sustaining economic growth. In the non-Western world Japan and Russia have clearly attained it. The phenomenal economic expansion in Latin America since World War II appears to have propelled Brazil, Mexico, and some other countries to this stage, and perhaps Argentina had reached it before Peron. A few other countries may have crossed the threshold from static to dynamic economies, despite continuance of low levels of production per person.

But India, Pakistan, Southeast Asia, Korea, China, most of the Middle East and Africa, and the more backward parts of Latin America face extreme difficulties in their efforts to industrialize. The great gap between individual incomes in these areas and those in Western countries is widening year by year. Communist promises seem more convincing in these areas than elsewhere. The industrialization of Russia seems to many of these peoples to be more pertinent to them than what happens in fabulous, faraway America. And propaganda about economic progress in China may be expected to have even more influence on Asians, especially if economic growth proceeds faster in Communist China than in non-Communist India.

Among the major problems impeding economic development in non-Western areas, capital shortage is perhaps the most obvious. It is acute in most of these areas except countries that have large oil income. India, to take the largest non-Communist country, simply does not have in sight the funds to finance its Second Five Year Plan, which is a program calling for only a small rate of economic expansion. India is, therefore, now calling for outside help in much larger volume than has been discussed heretofore. Nor are other areas likely to reach self-sustaining growth on the basis of domestic capital resources presently in sight. This situation suggests the grave conclusion that development by non-Communist methods in these countries will fail unless very large capital supplies can be imported. Proposals for a much enlarged flow of foreign capital have been voiced from time to time, but no serious discussion in Washington or elsewhere has yet provided hope for capital flows of the necessary new magnitude.[6]

India's problem is particularly acute. It is also particularly significant. Because of the profound political and strategic implications of the success or failure of India's attempt to develop within a framework of consent, India's problem poses in uniquely sharp form some unanswered questions about the ability of the West and the non-West to come to terms economically. As things now stand, India is attempting, through voluntary saving, taxation, and an imaginative and energetic village development program, to make the most of existing resources, including the idle time of villagers. India is also pioneering in the technique of democratic economic development planning. But it must be acknowledged that an impasse appears to have been reached, and that India is not generating the capital necessary for the projects planned. Foreign capital is required, and the only possible source of the bulk of foreign capital needed is the United States. As of now, the terms on which India is willing to accept foreign capital are not bringing forth the volume necessary.

There is a wide difference of opinion between West and non-West about foreign capital. While even the most complacent Westerners would scarcely regard as satisfactory the present status of the international capital markets, there still is a strong tendency for Americans to stand pat in our present views of what is right and proper. We believe deeply in private enterprise and have grown rich under it. We strongly advocate foreign private investment as the most appropriate answer to the capital needs of underdeveloped countries. American private enterprise abroad carries with it high levels of technical and managerial skills, thus providing in one package several of the elements most seriously needed by under-developed economies.

Non-Westerners, on the other hand, tend to be suspicious of private capital, especially if it is foreign, seeing in it exploitation or even a continuation or revival of despised colonialism. On government loans and grants, which are preferred to private investments, non-Westerners have difficulty understanding or accepting terms and conditions that we consider to be normal and appropriate. Intergovernmental capital is looked upon very favorably, and the International Bank for Reconstruction and Development (IBRD, the World Bank) is widely regarded as highly successful. But the volume of IBRD loans is very far below the total requirements of underdeveloped countries for foreign capital. Consequently these countries have pressed for additional international agencies for financing development. Of these the International Finance Corporation (IFC) has just started operations as a provider of equity capital. Efforts have been made, though not yet successfully, to establish a large fund of even more accessible international capital, particularly the proposed Special United Nations Fund for Economic Development (SUNFED). The total of international capital movements remains very far below needs, and neither West nor non-West has yet moved in ways that appear likely to increase the flow to a satisfactory level.

Capital, nevertheless, appears to be one major need of underdeveloped countries that may in fact be met to a reasonable degree. The great bulk of needed capital must unavoidably come from domestic sources. The underdeveloped countries today have as possible models the development experience of a number of Western countries, and also of Japan and Russia. In each case most of the development capital came from the developing country itself, although the United States, for example, received very important foreign investment. In addition to the possibility of emulating the successful domestic capital formation of such developed countries, the under-developed countries today have at least some hope that the international flow of capital will swell enough to meet their most urgent needs. There is a widespread awareness of capital needs, and the possibility appears to exist that they may be met.

Population pressure, on the other hand, poses problems of even more awesome difficulty to the most seriously overcrowded countries, especially India and China, but including certain other countries such as Haiti, or regions such as the island of Java. Here the models of the past offer very little comfort since they suggest at least a doubling or tripling of total numbers in the course of even the most rapid and successful industrialization. There are optimists who believe that such increases could be sustained, even by India and China. But at best, the requirements for science, technology, and capital would be prodigious in order to support population totals hitherto unknown and densities that have developed in the past only in the most highly industrialized countries.

Thus far, population experience in non-Western countries is repeating Western patterns. Death rates have yielded before modern sanitation and health measures, even in the absence of improved food supplies. Birth rates, on the other hand, are not subject to direct attack by modern technology but depend primarily on social forces and traditions. The tradition of a grim race with high death rates remains long after these death rates decline. In countries that have already industrialized, it is only after extensive industrialization and urbanization that birth rates have dropped significantly. These countries have usually had room for such population growth or, as in the case of European countries, outlets overseas for surplus people. The United States was singularly fortunate. This country had so much space that it could without difficulty absorb, not only the natural increase of the early settlers, but also the continuing inflow from the greatest overseas migration that history records. Successive waves of immigrants brought to our rich land a great wealth and variety of human energy, skill, and intelligence that contributed greatly to our growth. The social change that must accompany any successful economic development was fostered by the presence of these immigrants.

Thus population growth and movement did not notably retard economic development in the West, and in the United States and a few other countries they were major elements in the economic rise. But in much of the non-West today, especially in India and other overpopulated countries, population growth is a clear and heavy burden retarding development. The prospect in India is that the death rate will continue to decline as further progress is made in public health. But it does not yet appear likely that there will soon be a decline in birth rates, despite vigorous efforts by a few leaders to introduce family planning. Rhythm devices, contraceptives, and other methods so far attempted have not yielded significant results, and the much-sought oral contraceptive has not yet appeared. In the West the rise in population took place under circumstances where the additional laborers contributed as much as they consumed, or more. In India and China today, additional hands add to a labor supply already seriously underemployed, and consequently production does not tend to rise in proportion to the increase in people. This Malthusian problem is thus more difficult than any faced by the countries that industrialized earlier. If India is to industrialize without a doubling or trebling of total population, it will be by processes for which there is as yet no precedent. And China has already made a new departure in being the only Communist country thus far to acknowledge the problem of population pressure. Mao Tse-tung is reported to have stated in February 1957 that China could not afford any increase at all in its total of 600,000,000 people.

Other human problems than population pressure are many in both number and kind. Economic growth requires no less than a change in the way of living and thinking for hundreds of millions of the world's most conservative people. Acceptance of innovations, attention to disagreeable details, willingness to sacrifice part of today's very small income in order to permit larger incomes for children and grandchildren, co-operative effort by large numbers of people, even the attainment of simple honesty in business and government—all these and many other matters raise problems that in some non-Western countries appear, for the present at least, to be insurmountable. The Japanese clearly had what it took to meet these needs in the nineteenth century. The Soviet leaders of Russia have shown tremendous determination and have succeeded in imposing their will on the peoples of the U.S.S.R. and thus meeting these human problems up to a point, though at a human cost that appalls us. There appears no reason to anticipate that the Communist rulers of China will lose their hold on the Chinese people in the near future, although the news from China is filled with the mistakes and difficulties there. But in the non-Communist areas the willingness to use force is far less, and there remains much more question whether the necessary changes can be achieved in the very poor countries.

A final group of problems of economic development relate to international trade. The underdeveloped countries already depend heavily on foreign trade to maintain their economies, even without initiation or acceleration of economic growth, and this trade presents many unsolved difficulties. Economic development necessarily involves new trade. Natural resource limitations do not permit any country to be wholly self-sufficient at the desired higher levels of production and consumption. The capital goods necessary to efficient development must in most cases be imported by the underdeveloped countries. To obtain the funds to pay for such imports, underdeveloped countries must expand present exports or reduce present imports, except where foreign financing is available. Even with foreign capital, unless it comes as a gift, the developing country must still pay in exports, though payment may be spread over many years.

The present trade of underdeveloped countries consists, on the import side, of a large flow of manufactured goods, though a surprising amount of fuel, food, and other primary products are purchased abroad by underdeveloped countries. It is usually difficult, sometimes extremely so, to limit these imports of consumption goods in order to leave enough foreign funds for needed capital goods imports. Exports are mainly agricultural and mineral raw materials. The yield from these sales fluctuates violently, not in accordance with the needs of the exporting country, but from causes that are unpredictable and mostly beyond the control of the producing country. Both sales volume and price change from year to year, frequently continuing in the same direction for several years on end.

Such violent shocks as these would cause difficulty in even the best-managed and most resilient economy. But the underdeveloped economies are by no means generally well managed or capable of easily absorbing these fluctuations. High foreign exchange earnings cause high income in the exporting country, and the reaction tends to be an increase in imports of both capital equipment and consumer goods, including luxuries. When the downturn in foreign earnings comes, the underdeveloped economy usually finds that previously ordered imports continue to come in for some time, and trade deficits commonly become severe. Until a country develops rather far, a thoroughly rational utilization of such undependable foreign exchange earnings is hardly to be expected.

Brazil is an interesting example of many of these difficulties and also of problems relating to human factors and capital formation. To be sure, Brazil's economy has been expanding very rapidly and has a far wider margin for error than is true, for example, of India. Brazil's foreign exchange earnings depend to a large extent on coffee exports, and these are subject to violent fluctuations in both volume and price. Roughly two-thirds of total imports consist of raw materials, food, and manufactured consumer goods. The remaining one-third of imports is generally capital equipment. None of these major types of imports can be reduced easily in times of low export earnings, but most of these categories have a strong tendency to expand in prosperous years. The resulting pressure on the balance of payments and on the financial system is shown in severe foreign exchange restrictions, progressive inflation, and successive foreign exchange devaluations. In times of extreme exchange stringency it is sometimes impossible to import legally even such necessities as spare parts for imported industrial machinery.[7]

Yet the visitor to the capital city, Rio de Janeiro, cannot fail to be impressed—if not frightened or killed—by such manifestations of active import business as the large number of automobiles, busses, trucks, and combination vehicles that crowd the city. These are operated for the most part on imported petroleum. They careen madly through crowded streets in such disorder as to make daily living a dangerous sport. For the more timid there may be comfort in the sign to be found in many public vehicles, saying in Portuguese "God is my pilot." (In the Middle East, it is reported, similar signs say in Arabic, "Allah will protect us.") Man has made important changes in Brazil, as in the capital cities of countries far less developed. But man's control over his life—or death—is limited at best.

Brazilians share with the majority of non-Western peoples a strong dissatisfaction with many of the circumstances in which they find themselves. In the midst of recurrent shortages and breakdowns, or of unsold supplies and low prices, it is very easy for them to pay a good deal of attention to the obvious weaknesses of the international markets on which so much depends. Discontented with the terms on which their primary products can be traded for imports and with frequent violent market fluctuations, non-Westerners also bear a psychological resentment of their role in international trade. In their minds the production and sale of primary products is associated with poverty and colonial status, while manufacturing seems to be associated with wealth, prestige, and national power. These attitudes are very deeply rooted and cannot be expected to change quickly or easily.

Market stabilization, nevertheless, is not making much progress. The principal reason is the lack of support from the United States and other industrial countries. Our resistance seems to non-Westerners to lend credence to their view that world markets are controlled by the West in the interest of the West. Some efforts to control their export prices are being made by the producing countries. Brazil attempted to raise coffee and cocoa prices in the first half of 1957, and some effect was felt. But one producer, even Brazil, the world's largest coffee producer, cannot in most cases expect alone to raise prices for long. Other producers can in time provide any quantities of coffee and cocoa held off the market by Brazil in its effort to raise prices. Thus the feeling of grievance on the part of producing countries against the industrial countries continues and becomes compounded by a feeling of frustration.

Development of manufacturing industry is being pressed by virtually every country that seeks development. Industry is often sought in order to become less dependent on imports, both for prestige reasons and for the very practical purpose of reducing the pressure on limited foreign exchange incomes. In fact, to many people in underdeveloped countries, an outstanding objective of the development they seek is to make at home the goods of the

West—the cars, the cameras, and the myriad other products of modern Western life that are all too scarce in non-Western countries. Thus steel mills, hydroelectric power, and even highly automatic machinery are very prominent in development plans. Westerners who have studied economics are likely to warn that such facilities are quite inappropriate at the earliest stage of development, requiring large amounts of capital, skill, and time. These warnings are most often thoroughly sound, as in the case of the High Dam at Aswan that would require huge sums to be invested over a substantial number of years before yielding anything at all. The same capital and effort devoted to many smaller and simpler projects would yield returns much sooner and more easily, thus providing both more capital and more production facilities for further economic growth.

Despite such a dramatic fiasco as Egypt's Aswan project in 1956, industry is developing in some non-Western countries, and a major question is being posed about international trade as a result. Will the developing country be permitted to sell manufactured goods in world markets? Already certain low-quality Indian cotton textiles are underselling Western and Japanese cloth in parts of Africa. But Japanese cotton textile sales in the markets in the West are limited by many restrictions including "voluntary" quotas controlling Japanese sales in the United States market.

It is to be expected that developing countries will in time produce a growing list of goods that American and other Western consumers would accept if available. But industries threatened with competition from imports are loud in their protests, and these protests are often heeded in the industrial countries. Economists in the United States are having very little effect in pointing out that there is long-run economic advantage rather than harm to be gained by imports from developing countries; that low wages in foreign countries do not constitute a reason for interfering with trade but rather a sound basis for trade; that United States labor displaced by imports would tend to shift to more prosperous industries, including various expanding export industries, where wage levels may be higher and working conditions better; and that one of the most urgent needs in United States foreign economic relations is a large increase in imports into the United States. Other Americans who argue that we must import in order to improve political relations with other countries are having little more success in combating the current upsurge of protectionism.

The direction of economic development is thus toward maximum national and regional self-sufficiency, rather than toward a world economy characterized by specialization, trade, and high incomes. At present, foreign exchange shortages cause most non-Western countries to limit imports severely. Home production may in time alleviate some of the goods shortages, but the small size of the market for many products in non-Western countries imposes severe limits on the advantages of domestic manufacture. The Communist countries constitute one important trading bloc, and the emphasis on industry, especially heavy industry, in the major Communist countries fits fairly easily with general non-Western attitudes about directions of economic development.

This survey of the large problems of economic development in non-Western countries suggests certain conclusions that can be briefly stated. First of all the much desired increase in individual welfare is by no means yet assured in India and other countries with very low incomes. The problem of population pressure compounds the difficulties of development in a number of important countries. Because of Draconian methods, the Communist approach to economic development appears capable of raising production in China and elsewhere, though serious difficulties are occurring and individual incomes will not necessarily rise in the foreseeable future. Because of a widespread desire to throw off the "economic colonialism" of selling primary products in markets conducted mainly by Western people and buying in similar markets Western manufactured goods, non-Westerners may be attracted to the Communist approach to economic development, with its heavy emphasis on industry. The attraction of Communist techniques may well grow in the years to come if China seems to be developing faster and more successfully than India.

Of the three groups of problems discussed, those associated with capital shortage may, it seems, be met. There is no assurance, however, that India will get the foreign capital needed to meet the targets of its Second Five Year Plan. The West, especially the United States, can provide the necessary foreign capital, but so far both domestic capital formation and capital imports are far below needs in the poorer countries. Human problems are much more complex, and conclusions cannot be either so definite or so comprehensive. Each society that succeeds in making the transition to self-sustaining economic growth will do so by its own methods. In this realm the West has the least power to influence the general course of events, even though Western technology, advice, education, and other help can be provided. No foreign country can give a non-Western country the will, the discipline, or the societal means to economic development. We on the outside can have influence, especially if we are wise and appropriately subtle. But we cannot hope to control, least of all by the direct approach of telling a non-Western country what to do.

In the realm of international trade there are a number of very large problems, some not only unsolved but festering and promising more difficulty as time goes on. Here the action that the non-Western countries can take is far less than what is within the power of the United States. The failure to develop a vigorous and expanding free world economy based on growing specialization and trade, including trade in manufactured products, does not cause very widespread excitement in this country. But the protection of uneconomic home industries, being pursued in the United States with particular vigor in recent years, is being copied in many non-Western countries that are far less able to afford this luxury. They are putting scarce resources into making expensively at home things they could buy cheaply abroad, if they could be confident that they would be able to earn the necessary foreign exchange.

The economic foundation has not yet been laid for satisfaction of the rising expectations of most non-Western peoples. Both they and we have much to do if these foundations are to be established. This discussion should have made it clear that United States foreign aid, no matter how generous, cannot possibly solve all the problems of economic development. If we give aid and do nothing else, we make aid a substitute for sound policy. If, instead, we face up to the difficult issues, especially the issues of commercial policy, then aid can be an instrument of policy, one part of a total of United States policies that might make successful development much more likely than it now appears in India, Indonesia, and many other countries.

What is at stake is not just material wealth or comforts. Rather, the stake is the self-respect, the dignity, the health, the education, and the social progress of the majority of the world's people. We Americans cannot control what that majority does. We are less than seven per cent of the world's population. But economically we are much more than seven per cent. If we, who operate the world's leading economy, would take the lead in a co-operative attack on the problems discussed here, we might play a crucially important role in making the world not only more prosperous, but safer, more stable, and possibly more to our own liking.

Notes

1. For the area covered by the United Nations Economic Commission for Asia and the Far East, the Commission reports food production per person in 1955/56 to be 91 per cent of the 1934–1938 average (*Economic Survey of Asia and the Far East, 1956* [Bangkok, 1957], p. 179).

2. Gerald F. Winfield, *China: The Land and the People* (rev. ed.; New York: William Sloane Associates, Inc., 1950), p. 128.

3. United Nations, *Demographic Yearbook, 1955* (New York, 1955), pp. 740–749.

4. Figures quoted are gross national product per person. They are taken from U.S. Department of State, Office of Intelligence Research, *Comparison of Gross National Product, Consumption and Investment in Developed and Under-developed Countries*

(Washington, August 25, 1954). The figure for Japan is from Bank of Japan, *Economic Statistics of Japan,* 1956 (Tokyo, 1957), p. 318.

5. This formulation is adapted from various writings of Max F. Millikan and W. W. Rostow, especially *A Proposal, Key to an Effective Foreign Policy* (New York: Harper & Brothers, 1957), ch. v.

6. E.g., *ibid.,* p. 127; and *Economic Survey of Asia and the Far East,* 1954 (Bangkok, 1955), p. xiv.

7. For details see *The Development of Brazil,* Report of Joint Brazil-United States Economic Development Commission (Washington: Institute of Inter-American Affairs, 1954), especially ch. iv and sec. II of app. IV. The general problem of underdeveloped countries and foreign trade is more fully presented in two United Nations reports: *Instability in Export Markets of Under-developed Countries* (New York, 1952, Sales No.: 1952.II.A.1); and *Commodity Trade and Economic Development* (New York, 1953, Sales No.: 1954.II.B.1).

Science and the
Non-Western World

By W. ALBERT NOYES, JR.

W. ALBERT NOYES, JR., the Acting Dean of the College of Arts and Science and since 1938 Charles Frederick Houghton Professor of Chemistry at the University of Rochester, has also served as chairman of the Department of Chemistry and Dean of the Graduate School. He received his A.B. at Grinnell College and his Dr-ès-Sc. at the University of Paris. A member of the National Academy of Sciences, he has held a number of national and international scientific positions, including service as Division Chairman on the National Research Council, Committee Chairman on the Research and Development Board, and Vice President of the International Union of Pure and Applied Chemistry. He was President of the American Chemical Society in 1947 and has edited several journals, including *Chemical Reviews, Journal of the American Chemical Society,* and the *Journal of Physical Chemistry.* He participated in the drafting of plans for UNESCO and since 1952 has served on the United States National Commission for UNESCO. Author of many books and articles, he edited *Chemistry in World War II.* Among honors received in the United States, England, and France was the Willard Gibbs Medal of the American Chemical Society, awarded to him in May 1957.

SCIENCE is looked upon with hope and with fear by the peoples of the world. The hope is that science will reduce hunger, disease, and poverty; the fear results from the fact that it also provides means for material destruction and for the decimation of populations—means that are only dimly foreseen even by scientists and that arouse foreboding among the masses of people almost everywhere.

Learned men all too often fail to distinguish clearly between science and technology or to realize that social changes may result fully as much from an attitude of mind as from the provision of modern machinery. There is a vast distinction between learning to drive an automobile and knowing enough about science to understand the operation of an internal combustion engine. Persons trained in the fundamental principles of science are far more than technicians and mechanics. Their processes of thought and their approaches to problems should do more to affect the course of events than merely to provide the comforts of life. To overlook the cultural implications of mass education in science is to overlook the real cause for social change which will come during the next hundred years.

In attempting to assess the impact of science on the non-Western world we must perforce speak of those agencies, public and private, which are attempting to spread the benefits of modern technology to underdeveloped areas. But if we neglect the spiritual and cultural effects of a broad understanding of the scientific point of view, we will indeed run the risk of failing to understand the moral and social changes which are bound to occur in the years to come. Those of us trained in science believe strongly that its impact will increase general well-being, but for this reason we are often accused of adopting a purely materialistic outlook and of assuming that automobiles, radio, television, and air conditioning can—in and of themselves—make the world a better place in which to live.

It is necessary, therefore, for us to examine the broad implications of an increase in the number of trained scientists and engineers and of an education of the public in the rudiments of the scientific point of view. One cannot suddenly produce many trained men in a population that is largely illiterate. It may be evident to many of us that public works, public health, industry, and education should make it possible for tens of thousands of scientists and engineers to be used effectively in underdeveloped areas. But material progress must not proceed more rapidly than peoples can understand and appreciate it. For example, studies have been made of the social effects of improved housing. These studies tend to show that the provision of modern housing for families of an extremely low social stratum does not necessarily raise the standard of living at once. If families are accustomed to chickens in the living room, it is difficult for them to understand why chickens should not be kept in living rooms of modern apartments.

The Western countries might provide scientists and engineers for underdeveloped areas. We will not consider the financial and economic difficulties of paying these men and of purchasing machines. Let us assume that some pilot area is chosen for experimentation and that the Western countries would provide the necessary capital. Good roads could be provided, automobiles put on these roads, and the natives taught to drive these automobiles. Electric and other power could be made available and factories built. Skilled workmen for the factories would be needed. There would have to be executives, secretaries, and artisans. But who is going to buy the manufactured goods and with what? Skilled workmen, if they could be found or trained, might be paid wages which would permit them to buy the goods made by the factories, but the immediate provision of roads, automobiles, and factories would not necessarily affect either the happiness or the welfare of the population unless there were accompanying developments in education. Should the population have an ingrained mysticism or practice a religion that stands in the way of experimentation and the adoption of reasonable diets or measures for the public health, improvement in material well-being may indeed be slow.

One might, by dictatorial means, establish an industrial economy of sorts in a generation or so even in a non-

Western country with an illiterate population. It would be unlikely that in that same time one would create a great army of literary persons, educators, bankers, and scientists. The elements of stability for such an economy would be lacking, and the economy probably would have to function for some time under a dictatorship or a semi-dictatorship. If there are intellectual and spiritual values to be gained from the impact of science, they could hardly make themselves felt in so short a time. Indeed, a nation suddenly industrialized might be a menace to the world. Along with the acquisition of power, a sense of responsibility for the proper use of that power must be developed, or the seeds of self-destruction will be present. Japan did succeed in industrializing in a remarkably short period, but the Pearl Harbor attack and the ensuing Pacific War showed that much Japanese thought was still feudal. The Renaissance is generally considered to have affected mainly literature and the arts. But the Renaissance brought also the beginnings of modern science and technology. This has been beautifully pointed out by former President Conant of Harvard in his little book entitled *On Understanding Science.*

Even as late as the seventeenth century, despite philosophers and even great scientists in astronomy and mathematics, there did not exist any great body of exact scientific experimental data. Such data could not be accumulated until gadgets had been developed which would permit planned experimentation. The carefully controlled experiment which tests the validity of an idea is at the very root of modern science, and controlled experiments can be planned only in terms of the apparatus to carry them out.

Science has not flowered overnight. Chairs of science in European universities scarcely existed until the beginning of the nineteenth century, although it is true that medicine and pharmacy had been recognized as university disciplines much earlier. Engineering in the United States had its main academic start at the United States Military Academy and the Naval Academy. Research in science as a truly academic matter may be said to have started with the founding of the Johns Hopkins University in 1876.

Today an estimated 60 per cent of the students at the University of Paris are specializing in science. At the University of Rochester slightly over 50 per cent of the undergraduates are in science and engineering. I do not have corresponding figures on the universities of the Middle East and Asia, but the percentage of science and engineering students is certainly well below that in western Europe and North America. Well-paid positions for such graduates are few in number in a nonindustrial economy. The social standing of scientists and engineers is not so high as that of lawyers, physicians, and politicians. Thus there are economic and social reasons for the difficulty of training scientists and engineers in a country where the need for such professional men does not already exist. The approach of many non-Western peoples to modern science and technology is often seriously impeded by traditions that an educated man must not soil his hands or do manual labor. Arab students have arrived at modern universities, with servants to do the required laboratory work or even to play soccer.

When time is fully occupied with a bare struggle for existence, none will be available to cultivate the arts, literature, and science. It is difficult for some persons to understand why the benefits of science cannot be made available overnight to underdeveloped areas. We are impatient to cause developments in a few years which have taken centuries in the Western nations. There can be no doubt that progress will be more rapid with outside help than it could possibly be in a country which could derive no benefit from existing knowledge, but basically a social and intellectual climate must be created in which science and engineering can flourish. The effort must be made to raise living standards so that people will have the time and the energy to be educated. This effort need not do violence to deeply rooted customs and traditions. The great need is for teachers trained in this type of teaching. Properly speaking, adult education must come first and the education of children second. We will return later to efforts being made by the United Nations and its agencies in fundamental education.

There is wide disagreement as to the place scientific education should hold in the process of amelioration of living standards. It is impossible to teach science to those who are unable to read and write, but we offer the suggestion that training in science may be more important in freeing minds from bondage than training in law, economics, and political science. The very basis for science is a belief in the orderliness of the universe and in the fundamental relationship between cause and effect. This is not to say that all natural phenomena can be controlled, but it is to admit that when an unpredicted event happens there is something wrong with our understanding and interpretation of the events which preceded it.

Thus a firm belief in the basic hypotheses of science

will discourage belief in the supernatural and raise hopes in the minds of men that hard work along carefully laid out lines will produce more or less predictable results. This attitude of mind is so ingrained in the consciousness of most of us that it is now hard to believe that it was far from accepted by our ancestors not many generations ago. The ultimate effect of its acceptance by the teeming millions of Asia and Africa will be tremendous. It will lead, beyond question, to changes in religious belief and to an irresistible demand for material, social, and political changes. The understanding of the basic tenets of science by the masses will bring a revolution that may compress into a few decades the evolution which took several centuries in the Western world. There is, however, a limit to how far compression can be carried. We are dealing here with trends that, by modern standards, are very long range. Americans are all too prone to believe that a few years will suffice to establish democracy and free enterprise. They forget history too easily.

Having thus issued a warning against excessive haste, let us see what is being done and what may be planned for the future. We must assume an era of relative peace during which colonialism gradually disappears so that the underprivileged peoples are free to work out their own destinies with such help from others as will be accepted. The first step should be a much wider program of fundamental education. The term itself must be defined. It does not involve the three R's but is a simple program in hygiene, in nutrition, in the better utilization of available resources to produce more and better food and to reduce the incidence of disease. Each locality must be studied and the program adapted to its particular needs. The modest rise in living standards which can be accomplished by the simple applications of scientific methods will lead to a demand for instruction in reading, writing, and arithmetic.

A program of fundamental education was initiated by the United Nations Educational, Scientific, and Cultural Organization (UNESCO) with a pitifully small budget, about $50,000 a year. It could serve only as a training program to teach teachers who would then return to their home bases and spread the gospel. The fertilization thus started can be effective only if governments of underdeveloped regions are willing and able to finance this program within their own borders.

Since fundamental education is essentially nonpolitical, it has encountered little opposition, but the few hundred thousand dollars now being spent will not have much effect. If hundreds of millions per year could be made available, and devoted, selfsacrificing teachers could be found, a very substantial rise in general living conditions throughout much of the world would result in a very few years. This would still leave poverty and misery, but the result could well be astounding in arousing a demand for education.

The educational program started by UNESCO on a modest scale has been accepted gladly. The next step, however, is fraught with greater difficulties of a political nature. All countries, including our own, are suspicious of the indoctrination of youth with new and dangerous ideas. Control of an educational system must be vested in local authority, and great care must be exercised not to arouse opposition by radical departures. For this reason reading, writing, and arithmetic can be followed most easily by emphasis on the study of science. Literature, political science, economics, and fine arts should follow when demanded by public opinion and must be in the hands of citizens who are trusted and respected by their governments. To proceed otherwise will court opposition to outside interference which could well nullify the benefits that might accrue.

This brings us to one of the main points we wish to make. The United Nations and its specialized agencies are the organizations which must be responsible for the program of education in science. United States citizens sent as United Nations envoys at the invitation of a government will arouse less opposition than United States citizens sent as representatives of our own government. It is vital to avoid any implications of colonialism, of forcing acceptance of our political philosophy by others, or of sending technical missions until they can be gracefully accepted. Each member nation contributes to the budget of the United Nations, and it will accept a United Nations mission as one coming from a body in which it has a voice. The psychological aspects of this problem must not be ignored.

With these broad generalizations in mind we may proceed to state certain needs of the non-Western world and to survey rapidly the program for meeting these needs. We must discuss this problem realistically. The world does not desire to be cast in our image, and, in any case, we should not be egotistical enough to believe that we in the United States have obtained final solutions to all human problems. Possibly the greatest benefit to the human race would come from the removal of fear of economic disaster. I refer not only to the dangers of crop failure or epidemic disease in a preindustrial culture, but also to factors which affect the level of business activity and standard of living in a more complex society. In this instance we shall not consider war, since war lies in the political sphere with which we are not here concerned. Quite evidently the productive capacity of the United States was adequate to maintain a very high standard of living during the great depression of the 1930's, but factors bearing little relationship to scientific and technological progress led to mass unemployment and great human misery. The causes for this collapse lie beyond our competence. We say merely that science and technology had progressed to the point that such misery is not necessary.

Nature is not always kind, but neither is she always cruel. There will be variations in meteorological conditions that will affect food production in local areas. In our own country we are familiar with dust bowls in the western states and with occasional severe winters in the northern zones which lead to crop failures. At such times appreciable areas would face starvation unless reserves of food were available or food could be imported from more fortunate regions of the world. World-wide food production may fluctuate for reasons beyond the control of man, but such fluctuations are minor compared to the violent changes from total crop failure to plenty in local areas.

An isolated area unable to export and import food may, therefore, suffer changes in its standard of living due to causes beyond the control of the population of that area. The solution to this problem obviously involves economic and political factors, but better transportation based on technological advance and better adaptation of knowledge of agriculture are also vital. The economic and political factors are not our concern, for to some extent the pressure for solving such problems will be irresistible once technological advance is sufficiently great. The social changes introduced in the United States during the 1930's were demanded by the people because of their realization that such widespread suffering was not necessary.

The transportation facilities for backward areas must be improved before much progress can be made to alleviate suffering. To a certain point improvements in transportation may be made by human labor without machines. Recent wars have taught us that coolie labor, properly directed, can build roads and carry supplies for great armies, but real progress will be made only when one man's labor represents a high ratio of goods transported to personal needs. Thus trucks, trains, and airplanes operating over good roads, railways, and airfields respectively, must be available to all segments of the world's population. These in turn can be operated only if adequate sources of power are at hand. We may not have in the world today enough productive capacity to furnish the same ratio of transport facilities to unit population as exists in the United States, but the minimum needs of the world's population could perhaps be met if all factories producing motor vehicles, railway equipment, and airplanes were operated continuously at full capacity.

A more serious question lies in motive power for modern transportation. Oil and coal reserves are large, but they are not uniformly distributed. Since a country can import fuel only if it is able to export something in return, the power problem is a crucial one for vast areas. For example, locally available sources of power in western

Europe could probably provide not more than 40 per cent of the present per-capita power consumption in the United States. Even with full utilization of water power and other local power sources many areas of the world will not have sufficient power available to operate transportation facilities on the level of western Europe and North America.

Thus adequate transportation requires widely available sources of power. This problem is being intensively studied. Provision of adequate transportation, however, is only a beginning. All too often we describe the unrest in the Middle East in purely political terms, whereas modern transportation has done much to awaken the peoples of that part of the world to the realization that a hitherto-undreamed-of standard of living may be within their grasp.

There is an urgent need in these underdeveloped areas for improved sanitation, medical services, and production facilities. Here education comes to the fore, and quite possibly the era of transportation improvement and improvement in education must proceed concurrently to avoid serious unrest. This is a major problem for which the world effort seems to be totally inadequate. The main United Nations agency facing the education problem is UNESCO. With a budget of about $11,000,000 a year, only $1,900,000 of which is allocated to its Division of Education, UNESCO's effort along these lines is obviously infinitesimal.

It is true, of course, that the UNESCO budget for education is only a small fraction of the total world effort going into education of persons from the non-Western world. The universities of western Europe and of North America receive tens of thousands of students from these areas. These students are in many fields, including science and engineering, but there are personal tragedies connected with some of this training. When these trained scientists and engineers return to their own countries, they may face unemployment. Many have tasted the joys of scientific research and do not wish to return to countries which do not provide facilities for such work.

Here we face a problem about which scientists are far from unanimous in their opinions. Should research institutes be founded in the hope that the benefits of modern science will gradually filter down to the grass roots, or should all of the effort go into education of the masses in the hope that research institutions will eventually be founded? Actually both approaches must be used.

Possibly a reference to our own history might be useful, although the parallelism with the non-Western world must not be carried too far. North America was colonized by western Europeans, many of whom were well educated. It is remarkable that a college was founded within sixteen years after the landing of the Pilgrims at Plymouth. Great scientists, such as Benjamin Franklin and Benjamin Thompson (Count Rumford) did grow up in the colonies before 1800. Neither of these great men was really the product of the colleges of the day, although Benjamin Thompson attended a few lectures at Harvard during a period of slack business caused by the embargo just prior to the American Revolution.

The Constitution of the United States refers to the encouragement of science through the granting of patents.

The first presidents were in favor of the creation of a national university, although Congress never treated this idea very seriously.

The Patent Office is the parent of several of the scientific activities in the federal government just as the hospital service for merchant seamen was the start of the United States Public Health Service. Nevertheless the most important scientific activities of the federal government prior to the Civil War were in the field of exploration. These expeditions not only laid the foundation for the opening up of western territory but provided much scientific information about wild life and natural resources.

The basic problem of federal financing had to await two important events. The first was the Civil War, which solved after a fashion the problem of states rights. The second was the education of the public on the advantages to be gained from science.

The second of these was naturally a slow process. The great explorations, such as that of Lewis and Clark, did much to awaken public consciousness about science, but probably the most significant step was the Land Grant Act that was the basis for starting many of the state universities and agricultural experiment stations. This act was passed during the Civil War, and the immediate postwar years saw the establishment of many institutions, some of which are now classed among our great universities.

The Land Grant Colleges and the agricultural experiment stations were directly beneficial to the farmer and to the industries based on mineral sources. Thus science was brought down to the grass roots. Perhaps this was not the abstract science of the theoretician, but it was the kind of science easily understood by the layman.

Thus the education of the public through low-tuition colleges, through university extension, and through county agents must be considered one of the decisive steps that led in the twentieth century to tremendous popular support for scientific activities both in and out of government.

These lessons to be learned from our own history must not be forgotten in planning for the dissemination of the benefits of science in currently underdeveloped countries. The first presidents of the United States failed largely in their endeavors to give science an important place in this country because public opinion was not ready for such support. Success came much later when a proper foundation had been laid. So also education in the most elementary parts of science and a clear demonstration of practical advantages to be gained by the application of science must precede the establishment of great scientific centers in the non-Western world.

The program of UNESCO is, therefore, a realistic one. It delves into fundamental education, although on too modest a scale. It attempts through exhibits to arouse an appreciation of science in the masses and through its four Regional Science Cooperation offices to provide facilities for travel and exchange of information, not only for trained scientists, but also to aid in the solution of local problems that affect health and happiness. Finally, through a major project on the Arid Zone it is attempting to solve important problems of recognized importance to the common man. This is the analogue to our own agricultural experiment stations.

The Arid Zone Program was first proposed by the delegation from India at the Third General Conference of UNESCO in 1948. Arid land tends to create meteorological conditions which perpetuate the arid *status quo*. Actually the area of such land is slowly increasing, with serious consequences for agriculture and for the future of populations in these areas. Water supply may well be the factor that limits populations in large parts of the world.

The initial budgets of UNESCO for the Arid Zone Program were very modest indeed. They permitted little more than a few meetings of experts. Even these proved to have great value. Some plants and animals are better adapted to dry climates than others. Some areas have hitherto unsuspected ground waters. Many things can be done without great expenditures, but exchange of information can be of immense benefit, for the arid zone problems have been dealt with in a variety of ways in various parts of the world.

UNESCO was founded with high and somewhat vague ideals. We quote part of its stated objective as given in the Directory of International Scientific Organizations.

To contribute to peace and security by promoting collaboration among the nations through education, science, and culture in order to further universal respect for justice, for the rule of law and for the human rights and fundamental freedoms which are affirmed for the peoples of the world without distinction of race, sex, language or religion, by the Charter of the United Nations.

Even this quotation contains words and phrases which mean little to many people. But there were many intellectuals who saw in UNESCO a source of funds to further pet projects. The net result was a diffuseness of the program which tended to deal with multifarious odds and ends. Only recently has any success been achieved in stressing major projects that have some chance of concrete results.

At the Montevideo Conference in 1954 the Director General of UNESCO, Luther Evans, former Librarian of Congress, was directed to prepare programs for two major projects: (1) Scientific Research on Arid Lands and (2) Extension of Primary Education in Latin America (Teacher Training).

At the New Delhi Conference during November 1956 the two major projects were approved, and the one on arid lands was provided a budget of $183,000 for 1957. The second received a budget of $224,000. These are modest sums, but they will be matched by equal or larger funds provided by the various nations where activities are conducted. Thus there is a modest start on getting the scientific program of UNESCO down to grass roots. These major projects, together with other sums designed to help the trained scientists of the world, mean that UNESCO is having an influence greater than might be expected from the modest budget it has always had.

Two other programs of UNESCO have the characteristics of major projects. We have already alluded to fundamental education. Two centers are maintained, one at Patzcuaro, Mexico, and the other at Sirs-el-Layyan, Egypt. The first can admit annually 65 students for a 19-month course, and the second can handle 160 students for a 21-month course. The total annual budget from UNESCO funds for the two stations is about $450,000, and to this is added about $125,000 from other sources.

The other program which may be termed a major project is for the education of Palestinian refugee children, for which about $150,000 is allocated annually by UNESCO. The total annual budget for this program is about $7,000,000, and about 200,000 pupils are cared for in four different countries.

We need not at this time give in detail the history and the administrative structure of UNESCO. There are seventy-seven member nations representing diverse political philosophies, religions, and education, and it is gratifying that such an organization can function at all. Possibly there is here sound basis for optimism.

UNESCO is only one of many United Nations specialized agencies, and several of these deal with science. We should mention a few of these in passing:

1. The Food and Agricultural Organization (FAO) with sixty-eight member states (1953) and a budget of $6,600,000 (1955) is one of the best known. Few can quarrel with its stated objectives which are "to raise levels of nutrition and standards of living of the peoples, to secure improvement in the efficiency of the production and distribution of all food and agricultural products, to better the condition of rural populations, and thus to contribute to an expanding world economy." This agency was started in 1943 and was the first of the United Nations specialized agencies. It provides agricultural experts, deals with broad economic questions that affect agriculture, and attempts to co-ordinate international controls to prevent the spread of plant and animal diseases. There can be no question of its usefulness, but its functions must be mainly those of co-ordination and stimulation. Its budget is far too small to permit it to operate labora-

tories and indulge in large educational programs. The non-Western world stands to benefit from FAO.

2. The World Health Organization (WHO) with a membership of eight-five and a budget of $12,000,000 (1955) is also very well known. Its stated purpose is laudable: "The attainment by all peoples of the highest possible level of health." With modern transportation, epidemics are no longer of concern merely to one nation. A person infected in one country may circle the world not once but several times before he shows symptoms of disease. Thus every nation is interested in the health of all others. Not only does WHO concern itself with the spread of disease but also with general health, which affects the susceptibility of a people to disease. Quite naturally, doctors and nurses must be trained mainly in nations where medical schools and public health services now exist, but much can be done by very elementary instruction and by example. Local customs and sometimes religion often stand in the way of progress so that the world badly needs more public health officers with an understanding of non-Western peoples. Progress can be made, but it will not be rapid.

3. The World Meteorological Organization (WMO) with eighty-seven members has a budget of only $400,000. Weather forecasting concerns us all. It is vital to transportation, particularly by plane and by ship, as well as to many industries, notably agriculture. Since weather is no respecter of national boundaries, it is evident that weather forecasting demands international co-operation. The predecessor of WMO, the International Meteorological Organization, founded in 1878, offers the best example of long-extended international scientific co-operation.

Here the horizon is just beginning to become apparent. We know too little to forecast the future, but there is a vague realization that man may affect the weather. Possibly man will, in the process, prepare his own destruction, but there have been successful attempts to produce rainfall by seeding clouds, and it is known that vegetation will tend to produce a climate favorable to vegetation.

This, then, is an organization which deals with both short-range and long-range objectives. Its usefulness is unquestioned.

4. The International Civil Aviation Organization (ICAO) with a budget of about $3,000,000 (1956) and a membership of sixty-six nations (1955) deserves mention. It certainly deals with some scientific problems, but they concern mainly the industrialized nations of the world.

Finally the United Nations itself is concerned with the peaceful uses of atomic energy. Here is a field so vast and of such ultimate importance that we should give it more than passing mention. For the long-range future when fuel reserves will be seriously depleted, it would seem that our childrens' children may have to derive energy either from atomic energy via the sun or by more direct use of nuclear processes. Unless the quest for energy is successful, civilization as we now know it in the West will disappear.

Thus the United Nations and its specialized agencies are doing useful and far-reaching work, often with budgets that are pitifully small and inadequate. Ultimately these organizations should form the basis for the extension of science and technology to all parts of the world. But we must face realistically the fact that some nations contribute more than others to the support of these bodies. Payments by each country are calculated according to a formula based on population, on national income, and on the number of adhering nations. The United States share may be as much as one-third in some instances, even though we have only about 7 per cent of the population of the world. Since Communist China does not belong to any of these bodies, it might be fairer to say that we have about 10 per cent of the population of nations eligible to belong to the United Nations and its agencies. But, of course, the United States has more than half the manufacturing capacity of the world and perhaps an even higher portion of the world's ability to support international organizations.

It is much too early to judge the real benefits to be derived from the various activities that we have had space to mention only briefly. The growth of technical competence in the underdeveloped areas should be a sort of chain reaction whenever the elements for popular support have been brought together. In the absence of such elements progress may be slow indeed. Countries like Japan, China, and India already have many competently trained scientists and engineers, and in Japan the industrialization of the economy has proceeded quite far. Political and other factors have prevented similar industrialization in the other two countries even though they seem to be far more abundantly supplied with raw materials.

We must, therefore, be careful not to assume that the training of scientists and engineers will work miracles. We scientists are too prone to neglect political and other factors in dealing with living standards and general well-being. One cannot by scientific training alone overcome a long history of inaction and acceptance of what is. Scientists and engineers, once trained, must be willing often to work under difficult conditions at levels that may not call for the full utilization of their training. The engineer who tries to improve sanitary conditions in a primitive village may receive small pay and work under trying conditions. He may find, not only that nature is against him, but that the people themselves will be opposed to progress.

Thus one may say that a genuine self-sacrificing missionary spirit must pervade the native scientists and engineers in underdeveloped countries. If, as is usually the case in non-Western countries, only persons from upper social strata receive scientific and engineering training, they will not be apt to make the personal sacrifice necessary to do the greatest good in their own countries. In the United States the children of well-to-do families do not usually choose science and engineering in college. They are much more apt to choose fields where the training is less arduous and for which the financial returns are greater.

Until such time, therefore, as education is universal and students can go through a university, if they have the ability, regardless of the social strata from which they come, progress may be painfully slow.

Many incidents show that real progress is being made. The Regional Science Cooperation offices of UNESCO provide mechanisms for the exchange of information. This leads often to the solution of vexing local problems. The profuse growth of water hyacinths hindered navigation and the migration of fish in Indonesia. The problem had been solved in Burma, and information on the matter was made available through the Scientific Cooperation Office in Djakarta. An epidemic of cholera in Egypt was stopped by wholesale inoculations by material flown in by plane. Vitamin deficiency in India is prevented by eating whole instead of polished rice.

A catalogue of the benefits of science, medicine, engineering, and agriculture would be long but not very interesting. The material benefits of the applications of science and technology are obvious to all. But the change in mental outlook brought about by scientific training will bring about a world revolution in the next hundred years.

The impact of science on the non-Western world will, therefore, bring great changes during the years to come. The first changes will be material, in the form of better food, better health, more comforts, and more leisure. These first changes will arise from applied science and technology with the main guidance furnished either by western Europeans or North Americans or by persons trained in institutions in western Europe or North America.

Even before improvement in living conditions is attained there occurs a decrease in death rate and an increase in life expectancy. Thus one may confidently expect a contest to be waged in the immediate future between increased productivity and increased population. We already have ample evidence that this is the first effect of technological change.

There can be no question that science furnishes the means for enormously increased food production, provided, of course, relatively cheap sources of power are available. There is no sound way of predicting how large a population the world could support in comfort, but a world with standing room only might not be very comfortable.

We wish to stress again, in conclusion, one of the main points we have tried to emphasize. Material comforts are important, but even more important is the change in mental attitude which the general diffusion of the scientific point of view will make. This is an intangible very difficult to assess. In our own country we have a tremendous ferment which leads us to attempt to tamper with the economy, with social forces, with government, with education, with all phases of life. We may forget that the controlled experiment is hard to formulate and even more difficult to control. Hence tampering in these areas may lead to unpredictable results, but our willingness to make changes must be ascribed to a more and more widely held feeling that change is possible and that experimentation is desirable. We may not have well-defined goals, but we are accumulating statistics so that if disaster ever does overtake us, we should certainly know why and be able to show with figures how badly off we are.

Since much more than half of the world's population has still to learn to read and write, the scientific point of view will not have much effect at once. That it will be felt eventually is certain, and the ultimate changes in both the material and social structures of the world will be tremendous. We may look to the future with optimism even if that future contains many unknowns.

Social Adjustment
to Technological Innovation

By JOSEPH B. GITTLER

JOSEPH B. GITTLER is Chairman of the Department of Sociology and Anthropology and Director of the Center for the Study of Group Relations at the University of Rochester. He received his Ph.D. at the University of Chicago and has been on the faculties at the University of Georgia, University of Chicago, Drake University, Iowa State College, and Colorado State College. He was formerly editor of the *Midwest Sociologist* and edited the volume, *Understanding Minority Groups*. Among his other books are *Your Neighbor Near and Far* (with Lami Gittler), *Social Dynamics, Review of Sociology,* and *Reducing Intergroup Tensions.* He has done extensive research and publication in the fields of social change and the sociology of science.

IT IS fairly obvious that societies as complexes of social relationships based on collective habits, mores, and institutions never stand still. Voluminous data record the vast social changes that have occurred and are in the process of occurring among diverse cultures and societies. The task in this chapter is to analyze the interaction between technological innovation and social change. Technological innovation will here be defined as that factor which includes mechanical inventions as well as the host of tools and techniques derived from applied natural science.

This focus in nowise implies that other elements are not also significant in creating social change. Physicoenvironmental as well as biological factors have played important roles in changing society or societies. Man has always had to adjust to his physical and biological circumstances. Periods of drought, warm winters in normally cold climates, and dust storms—all may alter behavior in particular localities. Biological factors such as disease, death, population density, and prevalence of organic life exert their influence upon the pattern of social life.

It is possible to study social change from the point of view of each of these and many other frameworks. The school of thought, for example, referred to as geographic determinism, illustrates the study of social change as an adjustment to physical environment. It correlates climatic and topographic conditions with social changes. The "social Darwinists," on the other hand, have formulated a theory of social change based upon biological change. All these have a place in broadening our understanding of how societies change. We cannot here explore the relative significance of each of these approaches. Nor can we ignore the very major role that nonmaterial innovations play as potent and dynamic forces of social change. Ideological innovations, such as democracy, communism, and mass education, have also radically altered the structure of many cultures.

Thus, bearing in mind these factors, we turn to the significance of the technological ones. Earlier we defined the meaning of technological innovation. It should be useful to delineate social adjustment as well. Social adjustment will be used to describe the way in which humans and their interlocking systems of relationships react and adapt to technological innovation.

Let us also recall the nature of culture and the manner in which it functions. By general consensus in social science, culture is defined as the learned, socially sanctioned behavior of a people. In this analysis, culture is not used to denote enlightenment or refinement in taste, thought, and manners. These are subjective value judgments and of little scientific significance. For all peoples from the simple folk to the Western urban possess culture. All cultures are systems of collective habits learned under a variety of physical and social conditions.

A culture, therefore, consists of the acquired habits and values that are shared by members of a society. This sharing tends to be universal among members of a simple society. In more complex societies it is frequently limited, in part, to segments of the society. In our own culture people of the same sex, age, education, and economic and occupational status interacting with one another frequently resemble one another in their habit patterns and value systems.

Culture fulfills a significant function for human beings. It enables those born into a given society to adapt to their environment, both natural and social, by giving them forms of established and approved behavior. It also provides a backdrop for creative behavior against which the exploration of the new can be projected. In the arena of personality development, culture provides the yeast of growth. The knowledge of cultures provides significant insight into the tensions and maladjustments that occur when diverse cultures meet.

The learning process by which we absorb our cultural patterns of behavior is called by anthropologists the process of enculturation. Enculturation takes place with little or no awareness and it is only when we are faced by alternative choices of behavior that we may gain some insight into the values and behavior that we have always taken for granted. If a new mode of behavior is selected, relearning is required. In culture theory this act is referred to as re-enculturation.

In the area of value systems enculturation is exceedingly significant, for it is in his value system that man finds the satisfactions that his culture affords. Consequently, when we bring programs to people whose cultures are dissimilar to our own—programs designed to change their way of life in part or in whole—the tacit assumption is that our modes and our values will bring far greater rewards than their culture affords. We further assume that when we offer these new values and new rewards, people in other cultures will readily discard their own and accept ours with enthusiasm. These assumptions in the light of our present knowledge of cultural dynamics are highly questionable. Indeed, evidence to the contrary is accumulating each day.

In East Africa, for example, several regions have been noted for their excellence as pasture land. One of the drawbacks to the utilization of these areas for producing beef for export has been the presence of the tsetse fly whose sting was fatal to cattle. When a vaccine was developed against the fly a few years ago, it was envisioned that East Africa, rid of this scourge, would soon be able to supply the meat-hungry world with beef. All the favorable factors for such development seemed to be present. Natural resources would be put to productive use and an extension of the pre-existing economy would permit a rise in the standard of living by creating a cash income. It would also make a substantial contribution to a serious world need. It also seemed that it could be accomplished without the evils consequent upon detribalization and urbanization. Yet these expectations were not entirely fulfilled.[1]

The clue to this situation lies in the value system of

these peoples and its relationship to the substitution of new goals for those which have been a part of their cultural heritage. What role has cattle played in their culture? In East Africa wealth has long been measured in terms of the number of cattle owned. It has formed the basis of a prestige economy rather than a market-money economy. Social status is derived from the ownership of a herd. Cattle are regarded sentimentally, and they often form the theme of poetry and song. Killing cattle for food is exceedingly rare, and they are eaten only when they die or when the owner of the herd dies. The stimulus of a United Nations program for raising more beef did tend to raise the amounts produced and increased sales to some degree. It is recognized, however, that getting really substantial numbers to market will be a slow process since, for the natives, increased production simply increases the desire for possession; selling for money is still not a very meaningful goal in their existent value structure.

Manifold examples that could be culled from many other cultures would similarly indicate how complex the matrix of cultural patterns is and how significant these patterns can be in terms of the kind of adaptations people must make who accept totally different goals from those of our own culture.

Another characteristic of culture that has implications for the adjustment of peoples to technological innovation is its wholeness—the integration and interrelatedness of its parts. This is a fundamental proposition of anthropological science. The culture of a human group is no mere congeries of behavioral traits, knowledge, and belief but an interlocking and systematic entity. In effect, this would indicate that a change in one aspect of a culture would almost inevitably influence the other parts. It has been observed that a seemingly small change in some aspect in a given culture seems to threaten dislocations to the entire system or minimally requires relearning in regard to a whole series of customs and practices.

It should be interesting to trace briefly the myriad effects of a single innovation in our own culture and thus illustrate the way in which various facets of a society are altered by the introduction, adoption, and diffusion of a single invention. An excellent case in point is the automobile.

The manner in which this invention transformed the modes of transportation is obvious. It displaced almost completely the horse and mule as well as the manufacture of the appurtenances necessary for animal transport. In turn, cars, busses, and trucks greatly reduced both the passenger and freight services of the railroads. Characteristically, this innovation stimulated a host of other inventions and industries. To mention but a few will indicate the numerous ones that received direct impetus from the automobile. The oil industry, road building and grading, earth-moving machinery, motels, chain stores, and shopping centers—all created new industries and new habits of living.

The vast complex of population distribution which is so highly significant in establishing patterns of living was markedly changed. Originally, when people were highly dependent on horse-drawn vehicles, small towns and cities were clustered around the railroad stations and confined to relatively small areas. When automobiles (and rapid transit lines) became common, these quarters spread out far beyond the small central area. The suburban-urban complex as we know it today began to develop at this point, affecting economic patterns such as real estate, as well as the political structures of town, county, state, and national governments.

Schools and churches felt the impact. Consolidation of both rural and town schools became feasible, and along with it curriculum changes became possible. Many rural churches were abandoned, and long-established churches in the central city often gave way to new establishments in the area of the shifted population. Family recreation, courtship patterns, and friendship choices were all influenced by the greater mobility which the automobile provided.

This brief bird's-eye view of only a few of the effects of a single innovation is sufficient to suggest how closely various parts of a culture are linked and how an innovation tends to affect areas of human activity far beyond its specific purpose.

Now, while cultures are wholes, it does not follow that all cultures are integrated to the same degree and in exactly the same ways. Accordingly, we can expect that in a highly integrated culture the introduction of a new cultural element will have rapid repercussions on the total culture; in a less integrated culture the effects may only be partial.

We have already suggested that all cultural change begins with the process of innovation. It is hardly necessary to point out that a new cultural element will affect a culture only to the extent that it is adopted and spreads through the culture. Not all innovations are accepted nor are all innovations equally used. There is almost always some form of resistance to the acceptance and diffusion of an innovation.

Earlier we indicated how the traditional value system in East Africa created resistance to change. Let us examine some further illustrations. In Iran, where some agricultural practices are closely linked with religious values, an observer has pointed out that "to peasants who believe that raising chickens may call down a divine curse upon them, that planting vegetables may destroy fertility, modern agricultural technics are mentally inaccessible."[2]

In India, a Point Four agricultural expert reported that the farmers had been troubled by thousands of wild antelopes. The problem arose because the common name for these antelopes was *neilgai,* meaning "blue cows," and since cows are sacred to Hindus they would not kill them. In consequence they became a serious pest. They really were not cows, however, and a government decree was promulgated changing their name from *neilgai* to *neilghora,* which means "blue horses." Hindus then felt free to shoot them.[3]

Another example is the now familiar story told about the introduction of the telephone in a country in the Middle East. According to reports, the king wished to connect the capital with certain other cities, but the tribal chieftains would have none of it. The Koran contained no mention of the telephone, and it must therefore be the work of the devil. When, however, the king pointed out that the devil would surely be unwilling to transmit the words of the Prophet, and then had the telephone line carry the sacred word of the Koran, the chiefs were ready to accept the innovation.[4]

The recognition that some religious concepts and values are correlated negatively with scientific and technological enterprise received attention through the scholarly work of Max Weber, who focused his attention on the relationship of economic endeavor and religious belief. In studying Hinduism, Confucianism, Christianity, Judaism, Islam, and the societies in which they were found, he came to the conclusion that religious values and attitudes markedly influenced the daily activities and the economic structure of societies. More specifically, he suggested that the way in which a given culture interpreted the meaning of nature and the supernatural tended to determine its way of life. Weber's major thesis was that early modern capitalism and modern science came about through the new religious values of Calvinist Protestantism that emerged in the sixteenth century. A point of interest for this chapter was one of Weber's conclusions that classical Confucian China's rejection of science was due in large measure to "the magic image of the world" that pervaded its culture.

Tradition, itself, also acts as a powerful deterrent to innovation even when it is not linked with religious belief. Conservatism, or the predilection for the familiar and rejection of the new, seems to be universal. Men tend for the most part to cling to their old habits. The story is told about the reactions of a group of fellahin to the suggestion that a village pump be installed as a laborsaving device for the women. "You say that a pump will save our women effort and time. If that happens, what are they going to do with themselves all day long?" This was a serious dilemma, for in their minds it was not just a matter of saving time but a long-established dogma that it is a woman's function to carry water from the fountain.[5]

Another significant block to the spread of technological innovation is the character of traditional kinship structures in many cultures. In almost all preindustrial societies such structures are far more extensive and serve far more important functions than they do in our own society. An illustration of what is termed the "joint family" can readily be observed in both China and India. Such a family is much like a corporation and has continuity from generation to generation, there being no division of family property. Even when a member of the family does not live in the ancestral home, he is expected to contribute part of his funds to the common holdings, and in turn is entitled to support at any time.

With such a kinship structure, a change in economic procedures, which usually occurs with the use of modern technology is strongly resisted, since it would disrupt long-established family relationships. Characteristically, too, in such families, the oldest living male tends to be head of the household, and he is often exceedingly conservative in attitude. Even when some adaptation is attempted, the results are not entirely successful since the cultural value of taking care of all family members in a family enterprise regardless of competency is retained, and such a system is not wholly conducive to efficient management.

It can be said that, by and large, in any situation where there is opportunity for individual economic profit, the family ties of the extended kinship system will tend to weaken; conversely, the stronger and more integrated the bonds of the kinship system are, the more likely are strong resistances to modern industrial capitalism.

Still another source of resistance to innovation is the opposition which comes from the rulers or leaders in a given culture. In any social system, from the simplest to the most complex, those persons and institutions which possess power under the *status quo* will resist change that may threaten their power. Illustrations of this process can be culled in all societies throughout recorded history. Some colonial powers made effective use of this principle for a period by using and re-enforcing existent leadership to divert opposition to the introduction of new technology.

An exceedingly significant block to technological innovation has been the kind of age structure which is typical of populations in many of the underdeveloped areas of the world. In many of these countries there is a rapidly expanding population with a large number of children and a relatively small proportion of productive adults. In nations where there is a rather high degree of industrialization birth rates tend to be lower, and there is a greater proportion of adult producers in relation to dependent children. The former type of population structure creates many problems for technological advancement since children are nonproducers or at best inefficient producers when they are used in the labor market.

Since agriculture is so basic to the economy of underdeveloped areas, children are used extensively to work the family fields. This practice tends to impede the improvement of the labor force and keeps the standard of living low. Child labor comes only at the price of neglected education. As a United Nations report recently concluded: "Thus the people of the under-developed countries continually resort to wasteful exploitation of the oncoming generation of workers in their efforts to achieve a more adequate current standard of consumption. Their position is rather like that of peasants compelled by hunger to harvest their wheat every year before it has ripened."[6]

A very obvious obstacle to the adoption and diffusion of technological innovations is the widespread illiteracy and lack of technical skills among vast numbers of non-Western peoples.

Finally, resistance to change comes from xenophobia, or the fear of the strange. "In-group" members regard with suspicion both the people and the practices of "out-group" members. This has been observed and described throughout recorded history and can act as a serious deterrent to the acceptance of innovation.

While this brief summary by no means exhausts the resistances and barriers to the adoption of technological innovation, it has outlined some of the major ones. It would seem appropriate at this point to ask a crucial question. Can these resistances be overcome and, if so, by what means?

Culture, which we earlier described as being conservative by nature, does change over a period of time and from place to place. Resistances to innovations do give way under certain conditions. Some of the processes by which these changes occur are reasonably well known. Let us enumerate a few of the principles and propositions set forth by anthropologists and sociologists who have concerned themselves with this problem.

First, a recognition and an understanding of each type of resistance as it manifests itself in a given culture are, of course, the initial steps in overcoming it.

Second, and closely related to the first, is the need for a sound knowledge and understanding of a local culture; its structure and value system must be thoroughly comprehended in order to induce change successfully.

Third, technological innovations which bring with them products valued in the culture will be more readily accepted than those of little or no value in a particular culture.

Fourth, innovations which may upset the balance in the structure of a society must be carefully planned, and adequate safeguards must be introduced along with them in order to absorb dislocations and disorganization.

Fifth, wherever possible, technological innovations should be fitted into the existent structure; to the degree that they are, to that degree will they be accepted and diffused.

The foregoing are a few basic principles that should be helpful when the introduction of technological innovation is contemplated and should prove useful in mitigating resistances. The whole process is a highly delicate and complex problem which is possible of solution only when the multifaceted ramifications of the interlocking nature of culture are understood. The UNESCO projects are good case illustrations of the excellent work that is being done along these lines.

On the assumption that the barriers to innovations are lowered or reduced, what then may we expect in the way of changes that will occur in these societies?

Here we enter a highly speculative realm. Prediction in the field of human-social phenomena has always been a highly precarious undertaking. To quote such a prediction let us contemplate a statement by that cautious dean of science, Simon Newcomb, who attempted to forecast the future of the airplane in 1903:

There are many problems which have fascinated mankind ever since civilization began which we have made little or no advance in solving. The only satisfaction we can feel in our treatment of the great geometrical problems of antiquity is that we have shown their solution to be impossible. The mathematician of today admits that he can neither square the circle, duplicate the cube, or trisect the angle. May not our mechanicians in like manner be ultimately forced to admit that aerial flight is one of that great class of problems with which man can never cope, and give up all attempts to grapple with it?[7]

Yet in exactly eight weeks after this forecast was published, the Wright brothers made their memorable flight in a heavier-than-air machine at Kitty Hawk.

So we shall step in where sociologists and fools are unafraid to tread. We will protect ourselves to a degree by assuming that the effects of technological innovations in non-Western areas will follow along the general lines of the effects that occurred in Western societies. This is perhaps a safeguard, but that cautionary old proverb, "Better ride safe in the dark," should be heeded in this slippery arena.

What effects will technology and industry have on the demographic situation in non-Western cultures? The population problems in vast areas of the world are crucial ones. The first effect, and one that adds immeasurably to the difficulty of raising the standard of living, is a rapid decrease in the death rate, which obviously increases the size of the population. During the Industrial Revolution in Europe we saw this happen because the two major checks to population growth were gradually removed—

the lack of the necessities to maintain life and the almost utter lack of control of disease. It was primarily on these factors that Malthus based his theories. He failed to foresee, however, the possibilities of other forms of population checks.

These new checks are being used in many urbanized, technological societies; thus the reduction of the birth rate in specific countries in the West continues markedly. In those countries of the non-West where there are no prohibitive religious or social sanctions against contraception, we can confidently expect that a checking of the birth rate will occur, particularly where the death rate falls. Again it should be emphasized that this is an exceedingly complex problem the solution of which, although possible and indeed probable, is fraught with many stubborn stumbling blocks. A notable example of a country which has come to grips with just this problem is India, where a valiant government effort is being made to deal effectively with it. Although the attainment of the goal is not yet in sight, it seems not unrealistic to predict ultimate solution.

Closely allied to population changes is the development of urbanism stemming from industrialization. The presence of cities does not necessarily suggest urbanization. Urbanization is defined here as a ratio—urban people divided by the total population. The degree of urbanization can and does vary in any given region independently of the absolute number of people living in cities. India, for example, has far more people living in cities than the Netherlands but is far less urbanized. The underdeveloped areas of the world clearly are far less urbanized than the more technologically advanced areas. If we define preindustrial areas as those in which more than 50 per cent of the working males are engaged in agriculture, we find that only 9 per cent of their combined populations live in cities of 100,000 or over, whereas for industrial countries the figure is 27 per cent. The degree of urbanization increases sharply as industrialization increases.

One of the important social institutions in almost all cultures is the family. The effects of innovation on the family will serve to illustrate the many basic influences that occur in a societal structure. A somewhat naïve but charming comparison of the nonurbanized Chinese family as compared with our own, written by a Chinese student of anthropology studying in the United States, follows:

1) Among the Chinese you have the large family system; in America the small family system.

2) In China the largest number of families live in the country; in the United States the largest number live in the cities.

3) In China the grandfather or the oldest man is the center of the family; in the United States the wife and children are the center of the family.

4) In China, the oldest man is the most highly respected; in the United States the woman is most highly respected.

5) In China, parents are very kind to their children and take good care of them when they are young, but their children are expected to be very filial and support the parents when the parents are old and retired; in the United States parents are very kind to their children but their children are not very good to their parents and do not take good care of their parents when they are old.

6) In China the young woman works very hard in the home, but the old woman goes out to relatives or to visit the gods in the temples; in the United States the old woman

always works very hard in the home but the young girl goes out for a good time such as dancing, party, and moving pictures.

7) In China marriage is arranged by the parents or through a professional go-between; in the United States you have romantic love, free marriage, and arranged by the couple themselves.

8) In China you have the least number of divorce and desertion cases in the world; in the United States the largest number of divorce and desertion cases is to be found.

9) In China you have inequality between man and woman; in the United States there exists practical equality.

10) In China very few women are educated and they have no activity in community affairs; in the United States large numbers of women are being educated and their participation in community activities is considerable.

11) In China there is no birth control; in the United States birth control is practiced widely.

12) In China the children are trained to be polite and quiet and there is little provision for their recreation and play; in the United States the children are trained to be strong and active with much provision for recreation and play.

13) In China the clan is very important; clans are virtually absent from United States society.

14) In China there exists great ancestor worship.

15) In China remarriage very seldom occurs and is most shameful, particularly for women; remarriage for women in the United States is a common occurrence.

16) In China women are absolutely virtuous and submissive to the husband.

17) In China, unlike in the United States, kissing and petting seldom occur and are regarded as most shameful in young people before marriage.

18) In China there is very little contact between men and

women; in the United States contacts are many and normal.[8]

No extensive systematic analysis has as yet been made of the various factors which disintegrate the family-centered social organization and of the practices and values of the large family system. There are, however, exceedingly interesting accounts by observing travelers on the influence of the European and American family patterns on some of these systems. The contact of the Chinese in the cities with non-Chinese is said to have given early impetus to the disorganization of the large Chinese family. The emergence of the ideal of a national state in China involved a long period of struggle to shift a family-centered society to a state-centered one. Observers in China today indicate that this process still goes on. As has been pointed out previously, this change usually brings with it a host of other serious dislocations with the breakdown of long-established social controls. Crime, delinquency, family disorganization, and mental stress frequently follow in the wake of such change, particularly when it comes rapidly.

Space does not allow further speculation on the consequences of technological innovation on other social institutions. I think, however, that the outline has been sketched, albeit lightly, to give some picture of the myriad changes that are wrought in the entire life of a people when technology is introduced, adopted, and diffused.

There is one final point. I have implied throughout this discussion that innovation in non-Western cultures will take place through cultural borrowing or what anthropologists call diffusion rather than through original indigenous invention. This certainly does not imply that non-Western peoples are less creative or less capable than peoples of the West. Of all forms of innovation, cultural borrowing is by far the most common and important. The overwhelming majority of the elements in any culture are the results of this borrowing. Even modern American culture with all of its inventions has borrowed more than it has originated. As the world draws ever closer, we can expect diffusion among all cultures at an ever-accelerating rate.

Notes

1. Melville J. Herskovits, "The Problem of Adapting Societies to New Tasks," in Bert F. Hoselitz (ed.), *The Progress of Underdeveloped Areas* (Chicago: University of Chicago Press, 1952), p. 108.

2. Heshmat Ala'i, "How Not to Develop a Backward Country," *Fortune,* XXXVIII (August, 1948), 47.

3. Samuel P. Hayes, Jr., "Personality and Culture Problems of Point IV," in Hoselitz (ed.), *op. cit.,* p. 213.

4. *Ibid.,* pp. 213-214.

5. Margaret Mead (ed.), *Cultural Patterns and Technical Change* (New York: Mentor Books, 1955), p. 238.

6. United Nations, Department of Social Affairs, Population Division, *The Determinants and Consequences of Population Trends* (Population Studies, No. 17; New York: United Nations, 1953), p. 265.

7. Simon Newcomb, "The Outlook for the Flying Machine," *The Independent,* LV (1903), 2509.

8. Ernest W. Burgess and Harvey J. Locke, *The Family: From Institution to Companionship* (New York: American Book Company, 1945), pp. 37-38.

America Proposes, Asia Chooses

By CORNELIS W. DE KIEWIET

CORNELIS W. DE KIEWIET has been President of the University of Rochester since 1951. He is currently also President of the Association of American Universities. Born in Holland, he spent his youth in South Africa. He received his B.A. and M.A. from the University of Witwatersrand and his Ph.D. from the University of London, later studying also at the Universities of Paris and Berlin. He has taught in Southern Rhodesia, at the State University of Iowa, and at Cornell University, where he served also as Dean of the College of Arts and Sciences, Provost, and Acting President. He served for two years as Chairman of the American Council of Learned Societies, also as a member of the Advisory Commission on Underdeveloped Areas of the Mutual Security Administration. His writings include *The Imperial Factor in South Africa, A History of South Africa,* three chapters in the *Cambridge History of the British Empire,* and *The Anatomy of South African Misery.*

134

A FAMOUS allegory from Chuang Tzu, a Chinese poet of the third century B. C., as translated by Arthur Waley, goes like this:

It was the time when the autumn floods come down. A hundred streams swelled the River, that spread and spread till from shore to shore, nay from island to island so great was the distance that one could not tell horse from bull. The god of the River felt extremely pleased with himself. It seemed to him that all lovely things under heaven had submitted to his power. He wandered down-stream, going further and further to the east, till at last he came to the sea. He gazed eastwards, confidently expecting to see the further shore. He could discern no end to the waters. Then the god of the River began to turn his head, peering this way and that; but still he could see no shore. At last, addressing the ocean, he said with a deep sigh:

"There is a proverb which says,

None like me

Proves none so blind as he.

I fear it applies very well to myself . . . as I realise only too well when I gaze at your limitless immensity. Had I not this day enrolled myself as your disciple, I might well have made myself the laughing-stock of all who take the Wider View." [1]

Like all great allegories, this one is widely applicable. It is applicable to the history of the American nation, fed by a hundred streams till it spread from Atlantic to Pacific, till it seemed "that all lovely things under heaven had submitted to [its] power." But now we have reached a shore from which we see a world too great for us to dominate. Our great problem is to discover what for us is the Wider View, lest we be found blind. This wider view must first of all be seen by scholars, in universities. This volume is evidence of the reality of the academic conscience. It is already coming to be true that the finest body of experts in world affairs is being developed in America. If we are to understand the problems of our utterly interdependent world, we can only do so by recognizing the interdependence of the knowledge needed to understand these problems. Intellectually we face a most serious barrier that stands between us and an effective comprehension of the new world with which we have to deal. It is the rigid framework of Western experience in which we do most of our thinking. It is most difficult if not impossible to penetrate understandingly into the aspirations of Africa and Asia if we are formally ignorant of their history, their religions, or their philosophy.

For a number of years I have been a member of a committee on African studies composed largely of young scholars. These are young scholars who began to come into their own after the Korean War. Working with them has been a delight. Probably because their attention was focused upon Africa and Asia, they were less bound by the habits of mind of our older and more conventional disciplines. They saw the world freshly. Their minds were receptive to new formations. One day one of them gazed at the map of Africa and pointed out how little we understood the emergent Africa if we were guided by the political boundaries and territorial divisions imposed upon Africa by the Western powers. The arbitrary arrangements of the era of European colonization obscured and suppressed the ancient logic of climate, geography, soil, rivers, communications, and human habitation. Our minds, he explained, should be receptive to the expression of forces that did not make their discernible mark on political maps.

So we looked with free speculative eyes at our map. What new logic might be followed if the indigenous populations regained the initiative they had lost? Where a political boundary had cut closely related peoples in two, what new irredentism might develop in Nigeria? in the Gold Coast? in the Congo? Was it not in the cards that the whites in Southern Rhodesia, Angola, Mozambique, and the Union of South Africa would be forced into a tight defensive alliance, if the rising forces of African discontent pushed them too hard? Which of the great themes of Egypt's history was likely to gain the ascendancy—the theme of the Mediterranean or the theme of the Nile? If Nasser and his successors see their greater opportunity as the leaders of a militant Arab nationalism, then their front lines are in North Africa and Asia Minor. But Egypt is the Nile. Then should not the Nile be Egypt? If so, then the front line of Egyptian influence should follow the Nile to Khartoum, and then on to Lake Victoria. Maybe future

historians will set up Mr. Dulles' action on the Aswan
Dam as the beginning of the age of Egyptian Nilotic
imperialism. There is clearly a fluidity in Africa and Asia
which should persuade us to be very flexible ourselves in
reading and assessing the shape of the new future. I have
found it very useful to take out a historical atlas and turn
to the maps of ancient and medieval history in order to
rediscover the forces that were dominant in the times of
Pericles, Julius Caesar, Charlemagne, and the Crusades
and the age of Discovery. This habit gives a valuable per-
spective on the agelong relationship between West and
East.

During the extended historical period that Arnold
Toynbee makes the framework of his monumental study
of world history, power and initiative have been in the
hands of the non-Western world for a longer total period
than they have been in the hands of the West. By their
defeat of the Persians (490 B.C.) the Greeks became the
first European power in history to hold its own against
Asian power. Their naval battles opened the Mediterranean and its shores to influence and control from Europe.
The high point of this influence and control was reached
under the Roman Empire. But by the seventh century
A.D. the rise of Arab imperialism had reversed this relationship. Europe had lost control of the Mediterranean,
and the balance of power had once again shifted to the
East. It is a matter for controversy when European power
once again assumed the ascendancy. But Constantinople
fell in 1453, and in 1683 John Sobieski was defending
Vienna against the Turks. I am not trying to defend these
generalizations in any detail, nor saying that history re-
peats itself. What I am trying to do is to weaken the

thought that the ascendancy of the West is a law of history and irreversible. We must acquire the habit of seeing the relationship of West and East from *within* Indian history, Chinese history, Arab history, and very definitely Russian history. It may not be true that the balance of power between East and West has once again been reversed. But it seems very clear indeed that there has been a most remarkable transfer of initiative from West to East. When we use such terms as the power vacuum of the Middle East and the Indian Ocean, Arab nationalism, Chinese imperialism, the third force of India, Sudanese independence, or the Suez Canal crisis, we are describing the shifting power relationship between East and West.

At this point I want to say something about the problems of American foreign policy. Critics of American foreign policy, friendly or unfriendly, foreign and domestic, pro-Dulles or anti-Dulles, should always recognize that it is being conducted in a period of history when a complex transfer of power and initiative is taking place, when the peoples and governments of the non-Western world are each year less submissive to the authority of the Western world. The greatest weapons of offense and defense in history have not produced an equivalent strengthening of our diplomatic bargaining power. The traditional relationship between power and diplomacy has been altered. Our planes get shot down, our citizens are imprisoned, national interests are flouted, and we cannot, or do not, or dare not take those steps which would have been a matter of course in the nineteenth century. Dulles' notorious brink-of-war statement would not have been nearly so offensive or frightening in the generation of the Venezuelan crisis. The violent reaction against its use today is a measure of the restricted area of aggressive or forceful initiative left to us.

This is probably the single most important conclusion to be drawn from the Suez and Hungarian crises. We tend to keep them separate in our minds or to regard them as deeply unfortunate coincidences. But in one most important sense they have the same meaning. In one case the West retreated; in the other it failed to advance. It is an acceptable summary to say that the West, as represented by Israel, Great Britain, and France, yielded in the Suez crisis to the danger of Russian intervention, to the respect for non-Western initiative upon which the United States insisted, and to its own lack of self-confidence. The Hungarian revolt was a breach in the Iron Curtain. It was a potential beachhead within the Russian defensive system. It was the most obvious and open invitation the West has had to intervene in the satellite system of the Soviet Union, to try to exploit the weaknesses and hesitations which seemed evident within Russia itself. Not for a moment do I want to be understood as advocating this intervention, even though Frederick the Great, Bismarck, or Louis XIV would never have let such an opportunity slip by. All I wish to emphasize is that we did not act, that we allowed the Hungarian crisis to become an opportunity for Russia to reaffirm her position. By our inaction in Hungary and our insistence on withdrawal from Egypt we ourselves confirmed the existence of a line of demarcation between East and West beyond which we accept severe limitations upon our initiative. The ultimate recognition of Red China, which seems inescapable, will amount to a further confirmation and reinforcement of the implicit doctrine of allowing the people within the area in which Western power has collapsed or from which it has withdrawn increasing freedom to make their own arrangements.

For our own sakes we must reconstruct our university curriculums in order that the cultivated American can recognize the main themes of Arab imperialism, of Russian expansion, of Chinese thought, and African emergence. Let us take a simple illustration of self-deception resulting from inadequate knowledge. Since the war many Americans, some of them in the highest places, have felt that the growth of Communism in China was somehow the product of Russian intrigue, Chinese incompetence, and American bungling. This analysis gives Chinese Communism an accidental and avoidable character. It becomes possible to think about it as if it were both superficial and temporary and as if the nonrecognition of Red China was a proper attitude for America to take. I would not dare to predict what vicissitudes lie ahead of Chinese Communism. But I can warn you against the error of assuming that Chinese Communism is without deep causes and roots within Chinese history itself. We shall never understand Chinese Communism unless we know that a land known for the greatness of its economic crises entered in the twentieth century upon the worst economic breakdown of all its lengthy history. And then listen to these words:

The ruler's subjects . . . are incapable of taking long views. What they hate is toil and danger, what they want is immediate ease and peace, and they are too stupid to see that ultimate safety can only be secured by immediate discomfort and danger.[2]

Those who are in favour of giving the people what they want

and saving them from what they dislike are in these days called moral men; whereas those who are in favour of giving the people what they dislike and interfering with their pleasures are called immoral men. The facts are just the other way round. . . . If the people are allowed their pleasures, they will soon be suffering from the pains they most dread.[3]

It is a misfortune for a prosperous country not to be at war; for in peacetime is will breed the Six Maggots, to wit, Rites and Music, the Songs and the Book [of History], the cultivation of goodness, filial piety and respect for elders, sincerity and truth, purity and integrity, kindness and morality, detraction of warfare and shame at taking part in it. In a country which has these twelve things the ruler will not promote agriculture and warfare, with the result that he will become impoverished and his territory diminished.

Concentrate the people upon warfare, and they will be brave; let them care about other things and they will be cowardly. . . . A people that looks to warfare as a ravening wolf looks to meat is a people that can be used.[4]

These are somewhat random extracts from the writings of the School of Realists, whose political doctrines were actually applied in the fourth century B.C. Their code was amoral; their legal concepts were repressive; they denied the supernatural; they rejected tradition; they were totalitarian intellectually; they set expediency above principle; they practiced mutual espionage and invited a man's denunciation of his neighbor and brother. Little more needs to be said to make the point that historically and intellectually some of the practices of Communism are not as foreign to Chinese history as we have superficially supposed. In the fourth century B.C. the Chinese Realist philosophers saw the shape of a totalitarian society in a way more thorough and detailed than the West was to know until our own century.

We must expect at least a generation of turbulence and change in Asia and Africa. In this large and diversified area of "rising expectations" the incentive to positive action is far greater than it is with us. The new men, Mao Tse-tung, Nasser, Ho Chi-minh, even Nehru, Nkrumah, and Azikiwe, have to prove something. They have to prove that they can be successful. There is in them an incentive to action which is thoroughly understandable if we put ourselves in their position.

These men have an acute historical self-awareness, an understanding of their place in the stream of history, and above all a sense of the future, of possibilities that can be attained through effort and daring. They feel they have more to gain than to lose. When they contemplate the past, many of them have a sense of wrong, of grievance, of deprivation. One of the most sobering reflections which the thoughtful Western mind must face is that history, unlike religion, does not absolve men of guilt through contrition and penitence alone. There are sins to be purged and wrongs to be undone. Penances will be inflicted, sometimes harshly and unwisely. While it is true that the age of Western expansion was an age of beneficial development, it also contained within it slavery, the color bar, conquest, and demoralization. At the moment of renaissance in Africa and Asia there is a painful contrast in our attitudes toward important parts of the past. Much that we are willing and eager to forget non-Western leaders are just as eager to invoke to justify their leadership and enterprise. There is a passage in Alec Waugh's novel of a West Indian island where a completely Anglicized and highly gifted Negro reminds his white companion that at the heart of every relationship between white man and black man will always be the memory that one was once the slave of the other. That memory will never be wiped out. Freedom in the resurgent non-Western world is not merely freedom to embrace a new future. Sometimes it will be a freedom to exact a price for the past. What is most deeply moving about the feud between Israel and Egypt is that it is a feud between two states charged with the same intense passion about past wrong. They are so conditioned psychologically that they cannot make concessions to one another. We need merely mention Ireland, South Africa, Egypt, India, China, and Indonesia to recognize the meaning of this observation.

Here is the great difference between men like Mao and Eisenhower. Historically the United States has purged the grievances of the eighteenth century. It has conquered much and been defeated little. Its prevailing temper is one of repleteness and consummation. Out of such a context arise presidents like Eisenhower, concerned with peaceful international relations, the rule of law, and stable political frontiers. But a man like Eisenhower would be as wildly improbable in China as Mao would be in America. Upon Mao, and even upon a more democratic and western spirit like Nehru, there is a far greater compulsion toward action and performance. Not wealth but poverty, not repleteness and consummation but their opposite, mark the physical and historical environment in which these men think and act. In our own history we humorously contrast the Fathers and the Daughters of the American Revolution. The chips on the shoulders of the Fathers are not at all the same as the chips on the shoulders of the latter-day Daughters. These other men, the Maos, Nehrus, Sukarnos, Nkrumahs, Azikiwes, Ho Chiminhs, are the fathers of their revolutions. Only in Russia has the time come when the sons and daughters are taking the place of the fathers. This is obviously and seriously a transition of vast importance. The nature and outcome of this transition contains some of the answers to the great enigmas of today.

It is not inaccurate, then, to think of Asia and, increasingly, of parts of Africa as areas of unrealized ambitions, led by men of rising ambitions. By doing this we acquire a vision of a vast area in which there are many new centers of initiative and activity, from each of which can and will arise the problems that will keep our generation disturbed and anxious. It is important to say these things because many of us misinterpreted the nature of the postwar world. Immediately after the surrender of Germany and Japan in 1945 some of the most important decisions were reached on the basis of the conviction that the affairs of the world would be governed by the five great powers remaining in the modern world: the United States, Russia, Great Britain, France, and Nationalist China. The United Nations was built around this central assumption. Within very few years the collapse of Nationalist China and the obvious decline of Great Britain and France had reduced the five to two. At the time of the Korean War it seemed obvious that the affairs of the modern world were under the governance of Russia and the United States. It had become a bipolar world in which the confrontation of Russia and America was the dominating point of reference for every other nation. In a sense this was deeply true. But the stalemate between the two great rivals actually encouraged an opposite condition. It enlarged the area of opportunity for the new powers. After more than two years there is still considerable agreement that the Bandung Conference was one of the capital events of the postwar era. It was expressive of the self-awareness and the increasing self-confidence of what has sometimes inaccurately been called the Afro-Asian bloc. Since the Bandung Conference this self-awareness and self-confidence have clearly moved into the United Nations itself. This is indicated by the shift of emphasis from the Security Council to the General Assembly and by the competition between America and Russia for the adherence on critical issues of the lesser powers.

The causes of contention and discord no longer are to be found solely along the frontier that Russia and the United States have drawn between themselves. The most dangerous problems are in such places and territories as the Suez Canal, Algeria, the Gaza strip, Goa, Kashmir, Vietnam, Formosa, Iran, and so on. Wise students of the modern world no longer fall into the trap of making Communism the cause and explanation of the world's unrest in Africa or Asia. Yet at some stage in the analysis of any crisis, whether in Algeria, Indochina, Egypt, or China, it is imperative that men remind themselves that the primacy of Western thought and practice has been challenged. The intellectual fervor and the material success of Communism have provided the modern world with alternative and competitive methods of thought and action. The world in our era is making reassessments and choices in much the same way as do all great ages of revolution and transition.

Few efforts are more rewarding than the effort to see

through the eyes of a laborer on a Guiana sugar plantation, an Algerian nationalist, or a Malayan peasant living on the edge of starvation. The immense consequences of the Russian Revolution have created new opportunities for men to rise against the heritage of the past. It can no longer be taken for granted that the economic and political development of backward peoples can take place only under the influence and within the orbit of the Western world. The greatest change which the past generation has seen in Communism is its transformation into a massive and compulsive instrument to speed the rise of modern industry, to force inexperienced populations to accept a harsh and laborious existence in the service of industrialization, and to organize powerful political communities. When traditional systems are dissolved by the impact of the West and when populations are brought to a state of chaos without acquiring a new hopefulness about the future, the West itself paves the way to the Communist alternative.

Can we draw any conclusions that would be useful for the conduct of our foreign policy? If by conclusions we mean that we are looking for a formula to be simply and easily applied to the problems of the modern world, we are wasting time. There is no final formula.

Let me refer to another series of discussions on American foreign policy in which I have been participating during the past two years. In these meetings were scholars, government officials, and businessmen. They were a free and off-the-record discussion of the principal issues arising in the areas under the colonial rule of Western powers. Several of us, myself included, made the effort from time to time to emphasize or identify principles or governing themes for the guidance of our national policy. Should anticolonialism be the guiding principle of our African and Asian policy? In other words, to what extent should we as a matter of principle throw our influence behind the emergent peoples of Africa and Asia and to that extent dissociate ourselves from the so-called imperial powers? You will not fail to recognize that anticolonial sentiment has deep roots in American national history. I was reminded of this during an appearance before the House Foreign Affairs Committee on precisely this issue. I was deeply impressed by the degree to which a forthright and even aggressive anticolonialism seemed to some members of the committee to be the proper guiding principle for American foreign policy. In the minds of some of the members it seemed morally honest, politically sound, intellectually clear, and historically logical. They disliked the ambiguity of our foreign policy and thought nothing would be more healthy than the enunciation of direct, forceful, and consistent rules of conduct, so that we and everybody else would know where America stood.

In the meetings whereof I speak, several of us then raised the question, "Are there consistent, firmly held principles by which our foreign policy can be guided and which can be applied to the variety of issues that arise in Africa and Asia?" The effect was interesting and most revealing. My colleagues were men of great practical experience. Many of them were deeply involved in a practical sense. Some were impatient, some unhappy; yet all had an attentiveness that showed respect for the idea that principle might be invoked to guide our foreign policy. By some it was maintained that in the logical, consistent, principled meaning of the word the United States had no foreign policy. What we called foreign policy was a succession of ambiguous, sometimes conflicting, usually expedient acts which created the impression abroad of American dishonesty or confusion or inconsistency. There was final agreement that the United States did have a foreign policy. This policy did not enjoy the luxury of being based upon consistent principles. It was our foreign policy to be tentative, to accept the facts of expediency and ambivalence, to adjust decisions according to time and place—not necessarily to do or say about Goa what we did or said about Algeria, to take a stand in Vietnam that we would not take in Kashmir, to shift alternately between East and West, or sometimes just to stand still. Before we urge severance of colonial ties for Goa or Cyprus, we must stop to think about Hong Kong and Macao and about our own bases in Taiwan and Okinawa. Do we have principles? We believe in the progressive freedom and development of the peoples of Africa and Asia, but we know that the path to these is tortuous and beset by pitfalls. We have deep-seated convictions about colonialism and economic backwardness, but we have to deal with the attitude of metropolitan powers and the inexperience of backward peoples. We do not therefore identify ourselves completely with one side or the other. We sympathize with demands for political independence and economic maturity but try not to precipitate political crises.

Does this mean that we have achieved a shrewd balance between principle and expediency, that we know what we are doing and why? I fear not.

What, then, is the proper foreign policy for us to follow? The critic with no responsibility for decision or action does not find it difficult to criticize, but it is salutary and sometimes chastening to recommend, to try to make positive and creative contributions. It is in this spirit that I make suggestions. The cardinal principle underlying our foreign policy must be the maintenance of peace. We must recognize that today we stand where Great Britain stood in 1914. We cannot afford war. The avoidance of war is the main pillar of our national security. Any major war, no matter what its causes or purposes, is a major defeat. Yet this attitude has to be made compatible with the unpleasant reality that the world will remain agitated and riotous. To shrink from war does not mean that we can wrap ourselves around with our own pacific intentions. Therefore an important basis for our foreign policy must be an affirmative involvement in the affairs of the world. Part of that involvement is the maintenance of a high level of national conviction about the merits of economic and technical assistance, a willingness to endure ingratitude and misunderstanding, and a refusal to be provoked into withdrawal. In the sixteenth century there was a phrase: "Money is the sinews of war." In the twentieth century this must read: "Money is the sinews of peace."

It is also my feeling that it would pay us to modify our concept that we live in a bipolar world in which everything is conditioned by the deadlock between America and Russia. There are two steps that would go far toward bringing about such a modification. The first is a more deliberate policy of helping India to acquire stature and even a sense of profitable destiny in the non-Western world. This is gambling that India will become less resentful about the past and more hopeful about the future, that the pacific and democratic content of Indian history and thought will continue to outweigh the latent imperialism and autocracy in Indian life.

In the second place, my conviction continues to grow that we cannot wisely attempt to postpone indefinitely the recognition of Red China and its admission to the United Nations. Here we must practice what we preach and think more of the future than of the past. Admittedly we have much to forget. But our boycott of a government that seems firmly in the saddle and determined to struggle for its objective is less and less in our own interest. It is simple folly to sustain and feed a quarrel with 600,000,000 people and thus force them to use against us the initiative that we are powerless to take away from them. A large part of human history is going to be written by the Chinese people.

This has been another way of saying that we must realistically accommodate ourselves to the fact that there has been a revolutionary shift of power and initiative in Asia. The two revolutions that are taking place in India and China are likely to have a greater total effect on human affairs than the Russian Revolution of 1917.

While it would be a deep error to think too little or dismiss too lightly the moral and philosophic principles that always remain as a living force in our national life, it is true that our power to act and decide in the modern world is limited. If we do not wish to dominate others by the use of imperial power—if, in other words, we believe in self-determination—then we must recognize that the claims and aspirations of the Asian and African communities which we ignored fifty years ago are great. Indeed, their part in the making of the future will increase. This means that their share of initiative in the affairs of the world is collectively greater than our own, and the foreign policy of a great and humanitarian state like America cannot be successful or influential without the deepest understanding of the forces that arise in Africa and Asia.

Notes

1. Arthur Waley, *Three Ways of Thought in Ancient China* (London: George Allen and Unwin Ltd., 1953), pp. 55–56.

2. *Ibid.*, p. 212.

3. *Ibid.*, p. 214.

4. *Ibid.*, pp. 220–221.